TRUTH IN TENSION

---

55 Days To Living In Balance

DANIEL T. NEWTON

GP Publishing 2018

Contributing Authors: Annie Moyer, Kyleigh Koyanagi, Sebastian Smith, Jonathan Harding, Jonathan Carter, Aaron Fraga, Kim Egeland, Mason Prescott, Downing McDade, Eric Heinrichs, Daniel Fagot, Sara Fagot, Austin Chappell, Amelia Hossmann, Lydia Egeland.

ISBN: 978-1-7321660-3-5

DEDICATION

I would like to dedicate this book to my Grace Place Leadership Team, who went above and beyond to make my dream of being a published author a reality. I love you all!

TABLE OF CONTENTS

FOREWORD

I have known Daniel Newton for many years. He is one of the strongest mentors and innovative thinkers I know. He goes the "extra mile" in creating an environment for those he influences to experience truth and to feel valued at a high level. I have been challenged in powerful ways by his life and revelations. He lives on the cutting edge of truth, but because he is continually mentoring and connecting with others, he has found where people interpret these revelations in unhealthy ways. Those insights are the basis for his outstanding book, *Truth In Tension*.

Truth In Tension is a power-packed, succinct 55-day devotional that will help you think through some of the most important biblical doctrines so you can walk in them with long-term wisdom and power. His two-page format for each of the 55 truths is brilliant and easy to understand. Just glancing through the Table of Contents will let you know you are going to be exposed to some great teaching that will answer many questions most believers have wrestled with.

In my experience, both as a pastor and an itinerant minister, I have found how easy it can be for individuals (or even entire congregations) to veer to one side or the other on any given topic. The Word is filled with radical truths that sometimes seem to pull against one another and it's only when we engage in an active relationship with God that it all begins to make sense.

Holding the truth in tension, with your eyes on Jesus, will empower you to live a balanced and Christ-centered life.

Good job, Daniel. Every Christian needs to read this book. I highly recommend it.

Steve Backlund
Founder of Igniting Hope Ministries

INTRODUCTION

Truth is found in tension. When a single truth is magnified at the exclusion of another truth, we are left with an incomplete (and incorrect) perception of reality. In order to more clearly comprehend our world, truth must be held in tension. Living in balance is a necessity in a world full of mixed reviews. With the guidance of the Holy Spirit, we must take on a whole and unbiased view of Scripture in order to remain centered. Many people's greatest weakness is found in the overuse of their greatest strength. We hear something we like or find something we're good at and spin off into an extreme, with a narrow-focused zeal and excitement. If we exclude seemingly opposing truths, without weighing them into our thoughts and perspectives, we may find ourselves drifting, lost in a fantasy world of distorted reality. The goal of this devotional is to help you find balance in your own life. It's easy to step into an extreme without realizing it, but once you're faced with a supposed contradictory idea, tension is created, and *that* is where TRUTH is found.

On each page we'll take two truths and unpack their potential Biblical origins, the heart behind them, the extremes they can become, the scriptural balance between each pair of ideas, and finally how you can apply the newfound balance to your life. Here's the layout you will find on each page:

1. **Origin:** This section uncovers one of the potential Biblical origins of each truth being presented.

2. **Heartbeat:** This section explains the good heart behind a specific truth before it is utilized outside of its proper context. (Remember, deception is often merely a truth blown out of proportion.)

3. **Extreme:** This section shows the danger of over-emphasizing a single idea at the dismissal of another.

4. **Balance:** After listing the two extremes, this section will bring both of them into balance using Scripture.

5. **Application:** This final section will challenge you to examine your own life and return to balance, ensuring you don't use either extreme to become deceived and lopsided.

We pray that as you read this devotional, every day would be flooded with revelation light. We believe your eyes will be opened as you set your heart and mind on Jesus Christ. Let this book be an encouragement to you as you dive into the Word of God and participate in each day's application.

"I pray that the Father of glory, the God of our Lord Jesus Christ,
would impart to you the riches of the Spirit of wisdom and the
Spirit of revelation to know him through your deepening intimacy
with him. I pray that the light of God will illuminate the eyes of
your imagination, flooding you with light, until you experience the
full revelation of the hope of his calling—that is, the wealth of God's
glorious inheritances that he finds in us, his holy ones!"
—Ephesians 1:17-18 (TPT)

"And you shall know the truth, and the truth shall make you free."

—John 8:32

Day 1

Holy Lifestyle vs. Living in Grace

Holy Lifestyle

1. **Origin:** *"If you love Me, keep My commandments."* (John 14:15)
2. **Heartbeat:** Holiness is a result of truly loving Jesus. As we behold who He is our hearts will respond in devotion, sacrifice, and discipline. He is holy so we, too, should desire that holiness.
3. **Extreme—RELIGION:** If we are caught in religion we are "bewitched" (see Galatians 3) with the deceptive belief that our own efforts of holiness will perfect us and allow us to receive from God. This causes instability because we allow our own righteousness to determine our identity rather than Christ's.

Living in Grace

1. **Origin:** *"For by grace you have been saved through faith, and that not of yourselves; it is the gift of God, not of works, lest anyone should boast."* (Eph. 2:8-9)
2. **Heartbeat:** After reading Scriptures on God's mercy and grace, like the one above, we realize our identity doesn't come from our works. Grace doesn't look at what we do, but rather views us apart from our mistakes.
3. **Extreme—LAWLESSNESS:** Those who fall into lawlessness are led astray with the belief that what they do doesn't matter. It is true that works will not earn your salvation, but works reveal our faith (see James 2). If we live lawlessly, we will defile our consciences and ultimately misrepresent Christ to the world.

Balance: Relationship

John 15:5 summarizes this excellently: *"I am the vine, you are the branches. He who abides in Me, and I in him, bears much fruit; for without Me you can do nothing."* When we are in love with God, both religion and lawlessness lose their grips. As we commune with Jesus we receive His abundance of grace that actually empowers us to live in His holiness. Living in relationship with Him frees us from a "works" mentality and a constant striving to achieve righteousness, while also liberating us from the conscious and subconscious dominion of sin. Being with Him awakens us to the conviction of the Holy Spirit that guides us into righteousness. We don't need to live under the heavy weight of the law and, by God's grace, we truly can fulfill His commandments. All we need to do is come before Him with an unveiled face and walk with Him hand in hand (see 2 Cor. 3:18).

Application: Make it a goal to spend time with God every day. Come to Him with your heart open and ready to hear what He wants to say. Throughout your day, take moments to pause and turn your affection to Him, opening yourself to His guiding voice.

"Under the law, all you will have is religion, not a relationship with God. But God is after relationship with us, one that is dependent on His goodness and His goodness alone."
—Joseph Prince

Day 2

All My Sins Are Forgiven vs. Confession of Sins

All My Sins Are Forgiven

1. **Origin:** *"As far as the east is from the west, so far has He removed our transgressions from us." (Ps. 103:12)*
2. **Heartbeat:** God, through the finished work of the Cross, has clothed us with righteousness and wrapped us in His salvation. His victory at Calvary has removed our sins and made us new. The blood of Jesus has cleansed our guilty consciences!
3. **Extreme—NEVER CONFESSING:** If this is distorted and taken too far, we will start to think that we can do whatever we want without confessing or repenting from what we've done wrong. We eventually sear our conscience to the point where sinning no longer brings us godly sorrow.

Confession of Sins

1. **Origin:** *"If we confess our sins, He is faithful and just to forgive us our sins and to cleanse us from all unrighteousness." (1 Jn. 1:9)*
2. **Heartbeat:** As lovers of Jesus, we desire right standing with God. Therefore, we come to the light in confession and allow His blood to purge us of our sins. We leave nothing hidden from the eyes of Him who already knows all things.
3. **Extreme—ALWAYS CONFESSING:** When taken too far, this truth causes us to start searching our hearts, constantly looking for places we might not be in full communion with God. The focus shifts from loving God to self-perfectionism. We confess without hearing from God and eventually the relationship is

one-sided, where we are constantly confessing. In essence, we become the only one speaking.

Balance: Repentance

Having a repentant heart posture is the balance between both of these truths. When we repent we are changing the way we think and turning away from our sin. This doesn't have to look like weeping and mourning over our mistakes! It's about forsaking old mindsets and accepting a new way of comprehending, perceiving, and living life. Appropriate confession will come from a heart posture of wanting deep relationship with the Lord. *"Repent, then, and turn to God, so that your sins may be wiped out, that times of refreshing may come from the Lord" (Acts 3:19).* It's like any relationship, if you mess up, it's only appropriate to talk about it and make things right. At the same time, we must not let condemnation drive us into constant confession. It's possible to confess all day long without actually changing our minds and becoming more like the One we love! We need to see that confession is not the focus; knowing Jesus is.

Application: Is there something on your mind you haven't talked to God about yet? Give it to Him today! He's waiting with open arms to love you and give you grace. Know that the moment you repent, confess, and give something to the Lord is the moment that all things, yet again, become new. He became your sin so you could become His righteousness!

"God removes the sin of the one who makes humble confession, and thereby the devil loses the sovereignty he had gained over the human heart."
—Saint Bernard

Day 3

Nothing Apart from Christ vs. Everything with Christ

Nothing Apart from Christ

1. **Origin:** *"For all have sinned and fall short of the glory of God."* *(Rom. 3:23)*

2. **Heartbeat:** Genuine, Jesus-loving people see where they came from, faults and all, and desire to become a better version of themselves. They see that apart from His love, acceptance, and redemption, they are nothing!

3. **Extreme—WORTHLESSNESS:** We fall into an extreme when we mistake Scriptures like Romans 3:23, as expressions of our "worthless" condition. We run into error when we use our shortcomings as fuel to justify a low opinion of self. This unhealthy belief will lead to false humility and powerless living, which is a misrepresentation of the Gospel.

Everything With Christ

1. **Origin:** *"But you are a chosen generation, a royal priesthood, a holy nation, His own special people, that you may proclaim the praises of Him who called you out of darkness into His marvelous light." (1 Pet. 2:9)*

2. **Heartbeat:** This passage, and many others, inspire us to walk in the full inheritance of all that is ours in Christ as children of God. We see that we are of great worth and value as God's "own special people."

3. **Extreme—ENTITLEMENT:** We fall into entitlement when we believe ourselves to be inherently deserving of God's mercy and grace. We adopt a belief that we deserve what we've been

blessed with and that it's our "birthright" to have what we want. We forget that we were once nothing before Christ and that it is not by our own works that we've earned any of God's favor.

Balance: Sonship

"Therefore you are no longer a slave but a son, and if a son, then an heir of God through Christ" (Gal 4:7). We were once nothing apart from Christ. We were slaves to sin. But NOW, as sons of God, we are everything with Him. It's this truth that sets us free from both feelings of worthlessness and entitlement. When we know we are loved and accepted as a person, we will naturally live free from worthlessness. And when we understand that before becoming sons we were lost and wicked slaves, we will live free from entitlement. As we mature with a healthy sense of worth, knowing that we are no longer orphans in this world and that we can do all things through Christ, we will walk in sonship.

Application: Do you feel you are constantly getting down on yourself? Or do you feel like, in a sense, you *deserve* the grace of God? In either case, take some time to give thanks to God that though you were once a slave you are now a son or daughter. It's not because you deserve it, but because you are worth it to Him. God loved you so much that even while you were lost in sin He died for you (see Rom. 5:8)!

"Those of us who are regenerated to a new life God honours with the name of sons; the name of true and only-begotten Son he bestows on Christ alone. But how is he an only Son in so great a multitude of brethren, except that he possesses by nature what we acquire by gift."
—John Calvin

17

Day 4

In the World vs. Not of the World

In the World

1. **Origin:** *"[Jesus] said to them, 'Those who are well have no need of a physician, but those who are sick. But go and learn what this means: 'I desire mercy and not sacrifice.' For I did not come to call the righteous, but sinners, to repentance."* (Matt. 9:12-13)

2. **Heartbeat:** When we look at Jesus' life we see a man who was surrounded by the broken and sinful. We see a man who didn't ignore the world's problems but chose to immerse Himself in the midst of them.

3. **Extreme—COMPROMISE:** This goes to the extreme when we find ourselves desiring to be so relevant that we are willing to lay aside the truth of Scripture in order to stay connected with other people. We can even go so far as to let go of convictions and beliefs so that people will continue to like us.

Not of the World

1. **Origin:** *"Do not love the world or the things in the world. If anyone loves the world, the love of the Father is not in him. For all that is in the world—the lust of the flesh, the lust of the eyes, and the pride of life—is not of the Father but is of the world."* (1 Jn. 2:15-16)

2. **Heartbeat:** When we read the Scriptures on being set apart it inspires a heart of purity and sanctification. We look at the sin, compromises, and mistakes in our own lives and in the lives of those around us and we desire to make our lives a clean temple for Him.

3. **Extreme—HOLIER THAN THOU:** This goes to the extreme when
   we start creating a bubble around ourselves, ignoring the
   world's problems, and setting ourselves apart as its judge. We
   end up excluding those who truly need help.

Balance: In the World but Not of It

This is what Jesus prayed: *"I do not pray that You should take them
out of the world, but that You should keep them from the evil one.
They are not of the world, just as I am not of the world... As You sent
Me into the world, I also have sent them into the world"* (John
17:15-16, 18). Jesus was fully aware of the issues going on around
Him, yet He didn't run or hide from them; He chose to address
them. However, even in His assessment He had a heart full of love
and always followed the leading of the Spirit. Jesus desires us to be
in the world so we can change it, but we have to live from the
understanding that He first overcame it. John 16:33 says, *"These
things I have spoken to you, so that in Me you may have peace. In
the world you have tribulation, but take courage; I have overcome
the world."*

Application: Choose to examine the world around you but don't
merely look for problems; ask God for solutions. What activities do
you have lined up for today? Ask the Lord for wisdom on how to be
a light and a world-changer, even in the mundane of your
schedule.

*"The best thing this world can get is you being you,
with God all over you."*
—Bill Johnson

Word vs. Encounter

Word

1. **Origin:** *"In the beginning was the Word, and the Word was with God, and the Word was God." (John 1:1)*
2. **Heartbeat:** Jesus is the Word made flesh. When we know the Word, we are enabled to know God more intimately. It's important to possess a special love for the Scriptures.
3. **Extreme—GOD IS JUST A THEOLOGY:** When we focus so much on learning about God through the Bible without actually experiencing Him, we end up with only half of the relationship we are meant to have. God is not caught in a book and is certainly more than a doctrine or a theology. He is right here, right now!

Encounter

1. **Origin:** *"So the Lord spoke to Moses face to face, as a man speaks to his friend."* (Exod. 33:11)
2. **Heartbeat:** In our pursuit of God we know we are made to encounter Him. Relationships aren't established on merely knowing about a person, but experiencing what they're like as well. God is revealed through these encounters.
3. **Extreme—GOD IS JUST AN EXPERIENCE:** When all of our attention is given to experiencing a "fresh touch" from God, we have erred to an extreme. God is not here just to make us feel good. If we believe the chief objective of being a Christian is for

God to woo us, we've distorted the relationship into a vending-machine!

Balance: Relationship

"My soul longs, yes, even faints For the courts of the Lord; My heart and my flesh cry out for the living God" (Psalm 84:2). Relationship is the key to finding the balance between the Word and encounter. God has called Himself our Father, revealing that relationship is what He designed us for. If we have relationship with God, encounters will lead to a deeper knowing of Him, and not merely a "cool" experience. Likewise, when we have relationship with God, the Bible becomes more than a book to us; it's an invitation to encounter the very realities we read about. Relationship shows us that the God of the Bible is the God of the here and now.

Application: Spend some time alone with God today. Read His Word, expecting to experience and know Him more through the Scriptures. See it as an opportunity to know God more intimately and not merely another time spent reading the Bible.

"The soul can do without everything except the word of God, without which none at all of its wants are provided for."
—Martin Luther

Day 6

Hell Is Real vs. God Loves Everyone

Hell Is Real

1. **Origin:** *"But the cowardly, unbelieving, abominable, murderers, sexually immoral, sorcerers, idolaters, and all liars shall have their part in the lake which burns with fire and brimstone, which is the second death." (Rev. 21:8)*
2. **Heartbeat:** This belief is birthed out of a sincere conviction that those who don't know Jesus will ultimately have a future that involves judgment and separation from God in Hell.
3. **Extreme—TURN OR BURN:** This becomes an extreme when we place a greater priority on exposing the sin in someone's life, rather than their value. Jesus did not come to judge, but to save (see John 3:16-17).

God Loves Everyone

1. **Origin:** *"And He Himself is the propitiation for our sins, and not for ours only but also for the world." (1 Jn. 2:2)*
2. **Heartbeat:** Behind this belief is a heart that desires to elevate the goodness and love of God above everything else. We believe that His propitiation is truly sufficient for everyone's sin.
3. **Extreme—UNIVERSALISM:** This becomes a dangerous extreme when we forget that Jesus says that He gives those who *believe* the right to become children of God (see John 1:12). A person must choose to receive salvation from Jesus in order to be accepted as a child of God. We have the ability to reject Jesus and there are consequences for that. Universalism is a

rationalization that says: "Because God loves everyone, He automatically saves everyone."

Balance: Hell Is Real, Love Is Stronger

While Hell is a reality, it is not what drives or motivates us. God's love compels us. It is His goodness and kindness that leads us to repentance (see 2 Cor. 5:14 and Rom. 2:4). We must realize that, while Hell is real, it is not God's desire for any to perish, but that all would have everlasting life with Him. When we preach to the world, our focus should not be to scare them into Heaven with Hell's reality. His love is the most attractive force that ever existed. Display His love to others and they will be drawn into a relationship with Him.

Application: Do you feel you focus too much on Hell? Or do you absolutely never think about it? Well, there's a balance for that! We can't avoid that Hell is real when we look at the Scriptures, but that's no reason to fear it. Ask God to make you conscious of His love in this very moment. Give Him thanks that as a son or daughter of God you have the incredible privilege of no longer being bound by the reality of Hell!

"God proved His love on the cross. When Christ hung, and bled, and died, it was God saying to the world, 'I love you.'"
—Billy Graham

Day 7

Being Unique vs. Being a Follower

Being Unique

1. **Origin:** *"I will give thanks to You, for I am fearfully and wonderfully made." (Ps. 139:14 NASB)*
2. **Heartbeat:** Every individual is created uniquely in the image of God. Recognizing that there is no one like you is a crucial truth to believe. Celebrating each other's uniqueness is important, because it's the way God made us: many members of one body.
3. **Extreme—PRIDE AND INDEPENDENCE:** There is a danger when we use our uniqueness as an excuse to rationalize our behavior. For example, we will take the fact of how different we are to justify not being willing to fit in or adapt to a certain environment or group of people. We could use it to defend ourselves when being corrected, or even become prideful and not receive any feedback from people, responding with: "It's just who I am."

Being a Follower

1. **Origin:** *"Be imitators of me, just as I also am of Christ." (1 Cor. 11:1 ESV)*
2. **Heartbeat:** We are inspired by others' walks, lives, and accomplishments, and we look up to role models. It's important that we surround ourselves with great people and follow the examples they leave for us.
3. **Extreme—INSECURITY AND COMPARISON:** If we allow comparison to take hold of our hearts and move us beyond being comfortable with who we are, then we've stepped into an

extreme. We end up wanting to be a copy of someone else rather than becoming the wonderful person God created us to be. We will adapt, copy, perform, and strive to be like someone else but never find peace and satisfaction in who we are.

Balance: Identity

"And you, who once were alienated and enemies in your mind by wicked works, yet now He has reconciled in the body of His flesh through death, to present you holy, and blameless, and above reproach in His sight" (Col. 1:22). Who we are through Christ and His sacrifice is what should make us confident. We should not receive confidence from our own uniqueness or from following someone else's walk. God has created us in His image and our uniqueness is found in His purpose for our lives. As we discover who He made us to be, we need to know we are loved and accepted by Him (see 1 John 3:1). And while people should inspire us, mentor us, and lead us, Christ is the ultimate standard of our identity and where we find our security.

Application: Your goal in life should be to look like Jesus! Your identity comes from His love and not your own performance. It's important that we value our uniqueness, but it is also important that we adapt and grow more into His image by following the examples of those around us. Take a moment to write down three unique things about yourself. Then, write three other things you want to grow in that you see other people do really well. Now, take steps towards becoming uniquely identical to Christ!

"Anyone who has discovered who God has made them to be will never want to be anyone else."
—Bill Johnson

25

High Standard of Excellence vs. Resting in Victory

High Standard of Excellence

1. **Origin:** *"Therefore you shall be perfect, just as your Father in heaven is perfect." (Matt. 5:48)*
2. **Heartbeat:** Just as Jesus was perfect, we too, are called to be perfect. We understand that God has called us to a standard of holiness and with His Spirit we can truly walk in excellence.
3. **Extreme—PERFECTIONISM:** Those who fall into the trap of perfectionism will develop a fear of failure. This will cause them to hide their shortcomings in order to keep intact the facade of being perfect. Perfectionism leaves people feeling trapped in their mistakes and leads to condemnation over their inability to meet the mark.

Resting in Victory

1. **Origin:** *"They will come and declare His righteousness to a people yet to be born—that He has done it [and that it is finished]." (Ps. 22:31 AMP)*
2. **Heartbeat:** The truth of the Gospel is that Jesus has finished His work and every sacrifice demanded by God has been met in the body of Jesus. We are perfected by Him and in Him, and we can add nothing to what He accomplished. We can rest knowing that Christ has ultimately won!
3. **Extreme—LAZINESS:** We can become lazy when we misunderstand the Gospel and take it to an unhealthy extreme. We see the perfected and finished work of Christ and errantly think: "Because Jesus' work is finished, what is there for me to do?" This overemphasis generally leads to complacency and a

theoretical understanding of God that holds no power for living righteously.

Balance: Overflow

Colossians 3:23 in the Amplified says, *"Whatever may be your task, work at it heartily (from the soul), as [something done] for the Lord and not for men."* If you believe on the name of Jesus, you are considered perfect in Christ. It's from the overflow of this revelation that we can actually choose to live in excellence. When we live in excellence, we are living wholeheartedly for the Lord and not for ourselves (as described in the passage above). In all of this, we must see that it's no longer about us becoming perfect, it's about living from the perfection Christ has accomplished in us. Excellence says, "I am perfect in Christ. Therefore, I choose to live in this free gift of righteousness every day!"

Application: Is there a side you tend to lean to? Do you find yourself afraid of making mistakes or are you living in complacency? In either case, make this declaration over yourself today: *I am perfect because He is perfect, not by my works, but by His grace. I will live from that perfection today in order to bring glory to my Father in Heaven! Amen!*

"Living holy doesn't make God love you more, but it does increase your love for Him."
—Andrew Wommack

Day 9

Fasting vs. Feasting

Fasting

1. **Origin:** *"But you, when you fast, anoint your head and wash your face, so that you do not appear to men to be fasting, but to your Father who is in the secret place; and your Father who sees in secret will reward you openly." (Matt. 6:17-18)*

2. **Heartbeat:** Love is truly shown by action and sacrifice. Fasting is a beautiful way to deny our flesh and live totally focused on God. Fasting is often viewed as an offering to God, as a gift of love, or as a petition to God for breakthrough.

3. **Extreme—TRYING TO MOVE GOD:** This becomes an unbalanced extreme when we start to believe that our breakthrough will only come when we fast. If we forget that everything was freely given at the Cross, and we rely on our ability to "move God," we have become the achievers of our own blessing, provision, and righteousness.

Feasting

1. **Origin:** *"And Jesus said to them, "Can the friends of the bridegroom fast while the bridegroom is with them? As long as they have the bridegroom with them they cannot fast." (Mark 2:19)*

2. **Heartbeat:** We desire to celebrate His victory, so what better way than through breaking bread together! Feasting is a good way to connect with one another and enjoy the freedom we have in Christ.

3. **Extreme—SELF-INDULGENCE:** This can become a dangerous extreme if we begin living in self-indulgence. We also err when we start to judge those who do fast as "legalistic."

Balance: Grace Creates Works

In the book of James, the writer states that "faith without works is dead" (see James 2:14-26). Good works for Jesus are the proof of our faith. However, God's love and provision for us is not measured by how much work we produce, but by Christ and Him crucified (See Rom. 5). Fasting is important because it puts us into a place of total reliance on God and the provision of His Spirit; however it does not cause Him to move more. He already made the biggest move by sending His Son. Fasting and feasting should both be heartfelt responses to His unfailing love and amazing grace.

Application: What do you believe about fasting? Do you believe that your breakthrough will come if you participate in a fast? Do you think that there is no need for you to fast? Spend a few minutes with Jesus asking Him to reveal if there is any way that you have taken this discipline to an extreme. Ask Him if He wants to give you your breakthrough by a means other than fasting. If you tend not to fast, ask Him if He wants to reveal a part of His heart through fasting.

"The purpose of fasting is to loosen to some degree the ties which bind us to the world of material things and our surroundings as a whole, in order that we may concentrate all our spiritual powers upon the unseen and eternal things."
—Ole Hallesby

Day 10

Reliant on God's Spirit vs. Seeking Counsel from Men

Reliant on God's Spirit

1. **Origin:** *"But the anointing which you have received from Him abides in you, and you do not need that anyone teach you." (1 Jn. 2:27)*

2. **Heartbeat:** Jesus paid a high price to be able to come and dwell inside of us. We have the incredible privilege of having the Holy Spirit within us and He is the one who is ultimately responsible for leading us into the full knowledge of God.

3. **Extreme—INDEPENDENCE:** When we stop listening to the correction of godly leaders in our lives because "God is our only leader," we have crossed over into the extreme of independence. If we constantly neglect input from others, we are positioning ourselves for failure. This erroneous belief disconnects us from the Body of Christ and will ultimately lead to our own deception.

Seeking Counsel from Men

1. **Origin:** *"Likewise you younger people, submit yourselves to your elders. Yes, all of you be submissive to one another, and be clothed with humility, for God resists the proud, but gives grace to the humble." (1 Pet. 5:5)*

2. **Heartbeat:** We are called to be submissive to each other and to lay down our own desires for the sake of others. Being grounded in a godly community with strong leaders is a major component to growing in your Christian walk.

3. **Extreme—OVER-DEPENDENT:** If we find ourselves crumbling in our faith whenever we are apart from our Christian community, we have taken our reliance on others to the extreme. We will eventually develop fears around making decisions for ourselves and we may even subconsciously desire to be controlled by others.

Balance: Empowered Accountability

Living as a lone wolf ignores the fact that Christ set up His Church to function as a body (see 1 Cor. 12). However, we are also not called to be mindless robots who let others make decisions for us.

A godly leader is someone who calls others to walk in the full stature of Christ and helps them give account for their ability; this is empowered accountability. That's what we see Paul doing in 1 Corinthians 11, when he admonishes the church in Corinth to imitate him as he imitates Christ. Christ is our ultimate source, but we can't discount the people around us who are there to point us towards Him. We are called to be powerful people who are also humble enough to submit to one another.

Application: Would you say that you are more afraid of opening yourself to the input of others or of living without input? Ask the Lord to bring a godly person into your life to model empowering leadership to you. If you feel Him drawing you toward someone already in your life, take a step toward connecting with them on a deeper level today.

"If you're not accountable in life that means ultimately that your life doesn't count."
—R.C. Sproul

Day 11

Pursuing God's Power vs. Pursuing God's Heart

Pursuing God's Power

1. **Origin:** *"Heal the sick, cleanse the lepers, raise the dead, cast out demons. Freely you have received, freely give."* (Matt. 10:8)
2. **Heartbeat:** The supernatural is in God's nature, and because He lives inside of us, it should be in ours as well. Jesus set the standard for what it looks like to live a life of supernatural power.
3. **Extreme—IDOLIZING THE SUPERNATURAL:** We can take that desire into an extreme when we make it all about miracles and manifestations and lose sight of the Miracle Maker Himself. While the supernatural is real and exciting, it is not the goal of Christian living. We should desire the supernatural, but never worship it.

Pursuing God's Heart

1. **Origin:** *"Yet indeed I also count all things loss for the excellence of the knowledge of Christ Jesus my Lord, for whom I have suffered the loss of all things, and count them as rubbish, that I may gain Christ."* (Phil. 3:8)
2. **Heartbeat:** With a genuine heart to please the Lord, we make it our goal to simply know Him. We don't merely desire to see signs and wonders; we want an intimate relationship with our Maker.
3. **Extreme—DENYING THE SUPERNATURAL:** From a place of authentic pursuit, some have forsaken the miraculous in order to not get "distracted" from Christ. If we don't believe we are

called to a supernatural life, we can go so far as to think these manifestations are either evil or fake. If we think miracles and spiritual gifts were for people in the Bible but not for us today, we will miss a huge part of who God is and what He wants to do through us as His children.

Balance: Pursuing the Supernatural God

First and foremost, our focus should be to foster our relationship with the Lord and get to know Him for who He is—not just for what He can do in our lives. *"This is eternal life, that they may know You, the only true God, and Jesus Christ whom You have sent"* (John 17:3).

Out of this communion we find our true qualification and satisfaction, not through how many miracles we see happen. When we seek Him and know Him, we can't help but experience the supernatural. By believing in the goodness of our supernatural God we will see His nature invade earth and His nature is sickness-free and demon-free! The origin verse for ignoring the supernatural shouldn't frighten us, it should cause us to see that even with the supernatural our main objective is to know and be known by Him!

Application: Take some time to examine if your life involves the supernatural. If it does, ask the Lord that He would always be the focus of your life. If it doesn't, then spend some time with Him and ask Him to reveal Himself to you in His fullness... expect big things!

"The point of your life is to point to Him. Whatever you are doing, God wants to be glorified, because this whole thing is His."
—Francis Chan

Day 12

Healing Your Past vs. Forgetting Your Past

Healing Your Past

1. **Origin:** *"For I, the Lord your God, am a jealous God, visiting the iniquity of the fathers upon the children to the third and fourth generations of those who hate Me, but showing mercy to thousands, to those who love Me and keep My commandments."* (Deut. 5:9-10)

2. **Heartbeat:** In order to live with a clean slate and a clear conscience, we may desire to examine our past in search of anything that may be hindering our walk with God.

3. **Extreme—DWELLING IN THE PAST:** While the heart may be pure in it's examination, we must realize that God does not judge us according to our past, but according to the Cross. If we search our past apart from the leading of the Holy Spirit, we have stepped into an extreme.

Forgetting Your Past

1. **Origin:** *"But one thing I do, forgetting those things which are behind and reaching forward to those things which are ahead."* (Phil. 3:13)

2. **Heartbeat:** After reading such a Scripture we desire to forget where we have come from, realizing that Christ has become our new definition.

3. **Extreme—IGNORING ISSUES:** We take this to the extreme when we don't allow Jesus to bring up issues from our past that are still affecting the way we commune with Him. We need to be open to God leading us into wholeness. If we always avoid

34

facing our past, we may not experience how Christ has overcome it.

Balance: Allow Jesus to Bring up Your Past (If He Needs To)

"Go, call your husband and come here.' The woman answered and said, 'I have no husband.' Jesus said to her, "You have well said, 'I have no husband'; for you have had five husbands, and the one whom you now have is not your husband; in that you spoke truly" (John 4:16-18). At the conclusion of this story, the woman believes in Jesus as the Savior of the world and so do many in her city. When Jesus brings up her past, He doesn't leave her in her past, but rather brings her to believing in Him and His forgiveness. When Jesus brings up *our* past, He does not bring condemnation along with it. Instead, we develop a deeper relationship with Him and move beyond what we once were. There are some issues, however, that God empowers us to forget and simply move on from. No matter what, always remember: You are not your past!

Application: Which side do you find yourself on? Do you tend to look to the past to find out how you can "fix" an old sin so that your current problems stop? Or do you shy away from the voice of God that desires to eliminate a negative mindset rooted in a past experience? Simply pray the prayer that David prays in Psalm 139:23-24: *"Search me, O God, and know my heart; try me, and know my anxieties; and see if there is any wicked way in me, and lead me in the way everlasting."*

"The Lord opened the understanding of my unbelieving heart, so that I should recall my sins...and I should turn with all my heart to the Lord my God."
—Saint Patrick

35

Day 13

Fun-Focused vs. Task-Focused

Fun-Focused

1. **Origin:** *"A joyful heart is good medicine, but a crushed spirit dries up the bones." (Prov. 17:22 ESV)*
2. **Heartbeat:** Having fun and being light-hearted keeps you healthy. We shouldn't take ourselves too seriously! Jesus was anointed with joy beyond all His companions (Heb. 1:9).
3. **Extreme—NEVER FOCUSED OR PRODUCTIVE:** Living only for fun and pleasure deadens us to the fact there is great need in the world and we are part of the solution. If we don't spend any of our time being productive, our impact will be minimal.

Task-Focused

1. **Origin:** *"But I discipline my body and make it my slave, so that, after I have preached to others, I myself will not be disqualified." (1 Cor. 9:27 NASB)*
2. **Heartbeat:** We are called to live disciplined and diligent lives. Our mandate and calling from the Lord is no joke and it should be our ambition to accomplish what we've been put here to do.
3. **Extreme—LACK OF FUN AND JOY:** Maintaining constant focus on the need of the world without taking a day off will eventually manifest itself in either burn-out or health issues. We will become intense people, out of touch with both the greater world and also the very people we are desiring to impact.

Balance: Be Joyful Always

"Then he said to them, 'Go your way, eat the fat, drink the sweet, and send portions to those for whom nothing is prepared; for this day is holy to our Lord. Do not sorrow, for the joy of the Lord is your strength'" (Neh. 8:10). Whether we are having fun or being focused on the task at hand, joy is our everlasting strength. There are people who have fun all the time but still don't have joy! We need this immovable satisfaction that comes from knowing Jesus to be established in our hearts. When it is, then it won't matter how serious of a task we are given because at the end of the day, Jesus is still Lord. If we work religiously in hopes of leaving an impact on the people around us and we lose sight of joy, our impact will be shallow. If we forget to be joyful, we are forgetting about one of the most important gifts Jesus purchased for us. Life will not always be pleasant, but the Lord will always be pleasant toward us. It's important that we become very serious about joy; it is a key antidote that the world is looking for.

Application: Do you struggle with taking life too seriously? When was the last time you intentionally planned to do something fun? If you cannot remember, set aside an hour or two in your week just for that purpose. Bring along a friend you have been wanting to connect with. If all you have been doing is having fun, make time this week to share the Gospel with someone. Ask the Lord to show you the need in your community and how you can help meet it. The greatest privilege we have is representing Jesus to the world, both in rest and action!

"When our lives are filled with peace, faith, and joy, people will want to know what we have."
—David Jeremiah

Day 14

Divine Healing vs. Healthy Lifestyle

Divine Healing

1. **Origin:** *"But He was wounded for our transgressions, He was bruised for our iniquities; the chastisement for our peace was upon Him, and by His stripes we are healed." (Is. 53:5)*

2. **Heartbeat:** We believe that God is a healer and that, no matter what, He wants to make us well. With that in mind, we trust that God is greater than any sickness that could come our way.

3. **Extreme—NEGLIGENCE OF HEALTHY DIET:** If we are not mindful, we begin to believe that, because God cares for our health, we no longer need to care for our physical body. This thinking can lead us into a lifestyle of carelessness, gluttony, and overindulgence.

Healthy Lifestyle

1. **Origin:** *"Therefore, whether you eat or drink, or whatever you do, do all to the glory of God." (1 Cor. 10:31)*

2. **Heartbeat:** As God's own possession we have become the dwelling place of His Spirit. We are His temple! Keeping your physical body in check is an excellent way to give glory to God for the life He has given you.

3. **Extreme—NEGLIGENCE OF GOD'S POWER:** We step outside truth when we focus on natural health alone. Always getting caught up in the latest diets or health research can cause us to look to these things for our comfort and safety. We are deceived

when these things become our savior and source of life rather than Jesus!

Balance: Stewarding the Temple

1 Corinthians 6:19-20 says, *"Or do you not know that your body is the temple of the Holy Spirit who is in you, whom you have from God, and you are not your own? For you were bought at a price; therefore glorify God in your body."* In stewarding our bodies as the temple of the Holy Spirit, it is absolutely essential that we remember our reason for doing so: to honor God. Living a healthy lifestyle should not be done from a posture of fear and self-protection, but rather from a heart full of love for the Lord! We should not fear the research and health fads of our day, but rather walk confidently, trusting who He is in us.

Application: Start targeting health in your life today! Choosing to eat healthy and exercising is a powerful form of worship. It's a way of recognizing that our bodies now host the presence of God's Spirit. This can be practiced through simple activities such as scheduling regular visits to the gym or choosing to eat more fruits and vegetables. On the other hand, if you are finding yourself operating out of the fear that God will not care for your physical health, take this opportunity to commune with God and thank Him for the truth, which says, "by His stripes, we are healed" (Isa. 53:5).

"Jesus lifts us beyond the building and pays the human body the highest compliment by making it His dwelling place, the place where He meets with us. Even today He would overturn the tables of those who make it a marketplace for their own lust, greed, and wealth."
—Ravi Zacharias

Day 15

Receiving vs. Giving

Receiving

1. **Origin:** *"He who did not spare His own Son, but delivered Him up for us all, how shall He not with Him also freely give us all things?" (Rom. 8:32)*
2. **Heartbeat:** From a heart of childlike faith, we believe and receive from God all He has promised to us in Scripture. Jesus desires to be the source of our physical, emotional, spiritual, and financial wellbeing.
3. **Extreme—SELF-FOCUS:** We err on the extreme when we make this all about us. Self-focus will cause us to think only about what we can receive. This will create a selfishness in us that keeps us from living in generosity.

Giving

1. **Origin:** *"Give, and it will be given to you: good measure, pressed down, shaken together, and running over will be put into your bosom. For with the same measure that you use, it will be measured back to you." (Luke 6:38)*
2. **Heartbeat:** We earnestly desire to live life outwardly; focused on others rather than on self. Scripture declares that it is better to give than to receive (see Acts 20:35)!
3. **Extreme—GIVING OUT OF OBLIGATION:** It becomes unbalanced when we interpret Scripture from a wrong perception and start to believe that the extent of our giving will be the extent of what we will receive. That comes from a heart which does not believe the best about our Heavenly Father.

Balance: Giving out of What You Receive

The focus here is on our heart posture. John 15:4 summarizes this excellently, *"Abide in Me, and I in you. As the branch cannot bear fruit of itself unless it abides in the vine, neither can you unless you abide in Me."* We can only give out of an overflow of what we receive from God. We will only bear fruit to the extent that we abide in His love, as it's His Spirit which bears the fruit in us. We will live the Gospel in a self-serving way unless we allow His love to change us from the inside out. We give from the right heart posture when we have experienced the love and compassion of Christ toward us. That love we experience allows us to naturally live selfless lives.

Application: Your experience will catch up to your beliefs, so declare this over yourself: *"God would not have paid such a high price if I wasn't precious to Him. Even right now, I am receiving the love that God has for me into my being. I am loved because Love Himself is living in me. I am loved and accepted in the Beloved. I am the apple of His eye. I am wonderfully and uniquely created to love and to be loved. I have freely received, and I will freely give!"*

"If we are not full of Him we have nothing to offer to anyone else."
—Heidi Baker

Day 16

Godly Solitude vs. Thriving in Community

Godly Solitude

1. **Origin:** *"But you, when you pray, go into your room, and when you have shut your door, pray to your Father who is in the secret place; and your Father who sees in secret will reward you openly." (Matt. 6:6)*

2. **Heartbeat:** With a desire to know the Lord, we seek Him wholeheartedly in the secret place. We realize that God is our strength so we give our whole lives to encountering Him.

3. **Extreme—ISOLATION:** This becomes an extreme when we cut ourselves out from being a part of community, not giving any time to friends or leaders in our lives. We can end up spending all of our time pursuing God, not understanding that God wants to change us so that we can change the world around us.

Thriving in Community

1. **Origin:** *"For where two or three have gathered together in My name, I am there in the midst of them." (Matt. 18:20)*

2. **Heartbeat:** We understand that relationships are truly important and that being around people brings excitement and transformation in our lives. We know that there is an aspect of God that we can only see through pursuing Him corporately and we desire to see Him through new perspectives and teachings.

3. **Extreme—LACK OF INTIMACY WITH GOD:** This goes to the extreme when we stop pursuing God and become satisfied with our community and church events. We may even begin using

people to meet our needs instead of God which ultimately hinders us from loving like Christ does.

Balance: Giving from Overflow

The balance can be seen in Christ's ministry here on Earth. Jesus spent most of His time with His disciples and those who needed help, but He would often retreat away to spend time with His Father (see Mark 1:35, Luke 5:16, John 6:15). The true balance in our own lives is found when we go to God first to be filled and then pursue community so that we can give to others. When our relationship with Jesus becomes our greatest priority, it enables us to truly accept and recklessly love those around us.

Application: You are made to know Him and make Him known! If you feel like you spend all your time alone with the Lord, we encourage you to step out today and connect with a few friends. If you haven't been alone with the Lord in a while, we challenge you to make time for that today. He wants to meet with you!

"Do not imprison Christ in you. Let Him live, let Him manifest Himself, let Him find vent through you."
—John G. Lake

Freedom vs. Submission

Freedom

1. **Origin:** *"It was for freedom that Christ set us free; therefore keep standing firm and do not be subject again to a yoke of slavery."* *(Gal. 5:1 NASB)*

2. **Heartbeat:** After reading Scriptures like the one above, we desire to create an environment with no condemnation where people can truly be themselves and be accepted as they are.

3. **Extreme—NO CORRECTION:** As leaders, freedom can be taken too far when we create an environment without correction. We can shy away from correcting those we lead, for fear that we would subvert them to bondage like a master would treat a slave. Without correction, we end up with a situation similar to Eli's sons wherein the lack of correction left them with no regard for God (see 1 Samuel 3:12-14).

Submission

1. **Origin:** *"Obey those who rule over you, and be submissive, for they watch out for your souls, as those who must give account. Let them do so with joy and not with grief, for that would be unprofitable for you."* *(Heb. 13:17)*

2. **Heartbeat:** After understanding the passage above, we create an environment that emphasizes humility, submitting all of our lives to leaders and requiring the same from those who follow us.

3. **Extreme—CONTROL:** This can go too far when we don't empower those we lead to make their own decisions. When we

require them to only do as we say and never foster an environment of growth, creativity, difference, success, and uniqueness that allows room for failure, we actually cripple people rather than raise them up as leaders.

Balance: Empower into Responsibility

Balance is found when we lead by giving responsibilities within a relationship that has both submission and freedom. We are called to freedom and have been set free from the yoke of the law, but that freedom should be used properly and toward a selfless life (Gal. 5:13). Healthy responsibility in leadership comes with a balance: providing an environment of freedom while, at the same time, allowing leaders to make corrections along the way. This will give us freedom to be who God has called us to be while also setting us back on track to attain the goal of living like Christ. He corrects those whom He loves and, as leaders, we correct based on the identity of those whom we lead.

Application: Ask yourself, "Am I okay with people I lead seeing and doing things differently than I do?" and, "When I see a dysfunction in those I lead, is it difficult to correct them?" If you are struggling with control or freedom, ask God a dangerous question: "What are the thoughts you have towards the people I am leading?" Allow His opinion of them to change how you see them, and this will change how you lead them.

"Never tell people how to do things. Tell them what to do and they will surprise you with their ingenuity."
—General George Patton

Day 18

Slow to Speak vs. Having a Voice

Slow to Speak

1. **Origin:** *"So then, my beloved brethren, let every man be swift to hear, slow to speak, slow to wrath." (Jas. 1:19)*
2. **Heartbeat:** This Scripture motivates us to live in a quiet humility. It inspires us to drop our agendas and to patiently listen to those around us. In the heart of this passage lies a loving and intentional gentleness.
3. **Extreme—NEVER SPEAKING UP:** If, however, we allow silence to dominate us, we find ourselves in yet another extreme; never speaking at all! At the root of this belief often lies a self-conscious insecurity or a fear of hurting someone's feelings. We often mask these fears and insecurities and call them "acts of love or submission."

Having a Voice

1. **Origin:** *"For I am not ashamed of the Gospel of Christ, for it is the power of God to salvation for everyone who believes, for the Jew first and also for the Greek." (Rom. 1:16)*
2. **Heartbeat:** We are not ashamed to proclaim the goodness of God. With confidence, we should always look to share the message of Jesus Christ with those we encounter.
3. **Extreme—ALWAYS SPEAKING:** If we discover that our conversations are one-sided, with our voices taking precedence, we have entered into an extreme. This can happen when we allow our knowledge (or our agenda) to outweigh our compassion for those around us.

Balance: Patient to Listen, Bold to Speak

We should be humble and strategic in our responses to people. Our words are precious, and when we spend more time listening, we will both refrain from talking out of turn and have a greater understanding of the issue at hand. This empowers us to speak up with the solution! If we always speak we will never hear, but if we always listen we will never see life come from the fruit of our lips. We should humbly wait and listen, but we should also speak when it is necessary! Knowledge puffs up and love edifies (see 1 Corinthians 8:1). If we walk in love, we will be patient enough to listen and bold enough to speak.

Application: Think back over recent interactions with your peers, coworkers, or family. Was there something you wish you would have said? Was there something you wish you *wouldn't* have said? Whichever category you fall in, let the Lord do a work in you with His love. He delights in you, whether you tend to be quiet or outspoken. Declare this over yourself today: *I am patient enough to listen, and bold enough to speak!*

"Words which do not give the light of Christ increase the darkness."
—Mother Teresa

Day 19

I'm Perfect in Christ vs. I'm in Process with Christ

I'm Perfect in Christ

1. **Origin:** *"For by one offering He has perfected forever those who are being sanctified." (Heb. 10:14)*
2. **Heartbeat:** The truth of the Gospel is that we have been made perfect in Christ. He is our life source, our justification, and our righteousness. We are complete in Him and lack no good thing.
3. **Extreme—LIVING IN FANTASYLAND:** While it's true that Christ has perfected us, the perversion of such a belief can either lead to an emotion-denying lifestyle or a prideful outlook. If we deny reality (our mistakes, feelings, and circumstances) in the name of having been made perfect, we may overlook issues God wants to change.

I'm in Process with Christ

1. **Origin:** *"Being confident of this very thing, that He who has begun a good work in you will complete it until the day of Jesus Christ." (Phil. 1:6)*
2. **Heartbeat:** While we were delivered into the full measure of salvation, we do not yet see all that was promised. All of us have areas we desire to change or grow in. We recognize that Christ died for us, but we still have a great need to be conformed into His image.
3. **Extreme—INTROSPECTION:** Over-assertion of a desire for growth can lead to introspection. It is healthy to hunger for transformation, but it is unhealthy to be transfixed on the problem you want to grow out of. Furthermore, when we take on

the responsibility for changing ourselves, we become the god of our own world.

Balance: Christ Lives in Me

Galatians 2:20 says: *"I have been crucified with Christ; it is no longer I who live, but Christ lives in me."* Realizing that Jesus Christ lives inside of you is the key to effortless change! It won't be about pretending you are perfect, denying struggles, or partaking in a drawn-out process. It will be a life of faith where you depend upon God for your transformation. Christ has truly done it all on the Cross, but we need this to become a reality within us. Our process is realizing His perfection within us. It is realizing that we have died to sin and He is now our strength for righteousness.

Application: Regardless of whether you struggle to admit your mistakes or struggle to see past them, the solution is Christ. Pray this today: *Father, I give you thanks for the power of the Cross. With all of my heart, I need what You've purchased for me. I surrender my life into your hands. I cannot change myself apart from Your Holy Spirit, so I give myself to you and to your grace. Form Yourself in me today, I pray. Amen.*

"Spiritual growth depends on two things: first, a willingness to live according to the Word of God; second, a willingness to take whatever consequences emerge as a result."
—Sinclair B. Ferguson

Day 20

Scheduling vs. Being Led

Scheduling

1. **Origin:** *"Look carefully then how you walk, not as unwise but as wise, making the best use of the time, because the days are evil. Therefore do not be foolish, but understand what the will of the Lord is."* *(Eph. 5:15-17 ESV)*

2. **Heartbeat:** When we begin to value the time God has given us, we do our best to seize each passing moment. The desire to be highly effective in our daily life gives birth to an organized routine and schedule.

3. **Extreme—BOXED IN TO AGENDA:** We take scheduling too far when we stick to our schedule without wavering rather than making space for the Holy Spirit to lead and direct our steps.

Being Led

1. **Origin:** *"Most assuredly, I say to you, the Son can do nothing of Himself, but what He sees the Father do; for whatever He does, the Son also does in like manner."* *(Jn. 5:19)*

2. **Heartbeat:** As we grow in relationship with God, we desire to leave our time open, diligently waiting and actively watching for His direction in each moment. We end up stopping our routines to be available for His leading.

3. **Extreme—DISORGANIZED:** We take "being led" too far when the commitments we have made fall to the wayside or we find ourselves continuously late for appointments because we stopped to pray for someone or our time in the secret place went long.

Balance: Discernment in Scheduling

While setting out to preach the Gospel to the ends of the Earth, Paul had a plan for each journey he took. Paul set out to preach in Asia, but the Spirit of God intervened and in the night he received a vision of a man in Macedonia (see Acts 16). Man makes plans, but God directs his steps. We make our schedules and commitments, but allow God to intervene as well. When changing our commitments, the key is asking to be released and holding true to our word. If we feel that God is constantly trying to have us move against our commitments, we are not seeing the fullness that God works within structure, i.e. the Church and the Kingdom. Jesus says that our "yes" should be "yes" and our "no" should be "no" (see Matt. 5:37). He honors our commitments, but reserves the right to intervene.

Application: If you find yourself relying on your schedule too much, spend time asking God if there is anything he wants to interrupt your schedule with. If you never follow a calendar, schedule out your next 3 days and stick with it!

"A man working without this unction, a man working without this anointing, a man working without the Holy Ghost upon him, is losing time after all."
—D.L. Moody

Day 21

God Did It vs. The Devil Did It

God Did It

1. **Origin:** *"For the Lord disciplines the one he loves, and chastises every son whom he receives." (Heb. 12:6)*
2. **Heartbeat:** Parents discipline their children in order to set them up for success. God works the same way. He is a good Father and He disciplines us out of a heart of love, because His desire is to mold us more into His image.
3. **Extreme—GOD IS ANGRY:** We are out of balance when we start seeing everything bad in our lives as God's will or discipline. Believing that God gives us sickness, ushers in suffering, and puts evil on us to "grow us" undermines our confidence to come before Him boldly in prayer. We begin to adopt a view of an angry God who's "out to get us."

The Devil Did It

1. **Origin:** *"The thief does not come except to steal, and to kill, and to destroy. I have come that they may have life, and that they may have it more abundantly." (Jn. 10:10)*
2. **Heartbeat:** The devil wants to wreak havoc on every human, whether you are a Christian or not. He hates the fact that we are made in the image of God and he does everything he can to distort that image.
3. **Extreme—DEVIL-CONSCIOUS:** We are caught in the extreme when we erroneously blame every minor detail on the devil as though he is somehow omnipresent and omnipotent. This

creates a victim mentality and instead of focusing on the power of Christ that lives inside of us, we live a devil-focused life.

Balance: What Do We Partner With

"Keep your heart with all diligence, for out of it spring the issues of life" (Prov. 4:23). People often want to blame God or the devil for the various circumstances of life. However, we need to realize that so much of what happens in our lives comes down to our own decisions. The devil can only work with what you give him, and God doesn't want enslaved robots. Both cases require a partnership from our own hearts. We can partner with the devil, or we can partner with God. We need to take responsibility in what we want our lives to look like. We can't just flippantly point the finger at God or the devil when trials come. God wants to richly bless you in every way, but He needs your heart opened wide as a landing strip for His goodness.

Application: Pray this prayer today: *"Lord I repent if there are any areas in my life where I have believed that You were the author of pain and sorrow. You are a good Father and You only have good things for me. Thank You that You renew my mind with truth; that through Christ everything is possible and we are more than conquerors, because the enemy is under Your feet."*

"I'm not afraid of the devil. The devil can handle me—he's got judo I never heard of. But he can't handle the One to whom I'm joined; he can't handle the One to whom I'm united; he can't handle the One whose nature dwells in my nature."
—A. W. Tozer

Day 22

Knowing Who You Are vs. Knowing Who He Is

Knowing Who You Are

1. **Origin:** *"For by one offering He has perfected forever those who are being sanctified." (Heb. 10:14)*
2. **Heartbeat:** We become sons and daughters of God as soon as we receive Jesus. Our Father is the creator of the universe, and we have access to all things through Him. We are righteous through our faith in Jesus Christ.
3. **Extreme—PRIDE:** Throughout Scripture, we are shown our identity in Christ. However, we err on being prideful when we think that we are invincible and entitled to do anything that we want because of our righteous and perfect standing in Him. This may lead us to having the perception that we are sufficient in ourselves and can do whatever we want, whenever we want.

Knowing Who He Is

1. **Origin:** *"Because it is written, 'Be holy, for I am holy.'" (1 Pet. 1:16)*
2. **Heartbeat:** God is holy and has marked His people for holiness. When you receive His Spirit it is only natural to desire a holy lifestyle.
3. **Extreme—CONDEMNATION:** When we serve such a holy God it can be easy to beat ourselves up when we don't feel we measure up. Condemnation creeps its way in when we believe our holiness is dependent upon our own ability rather than God's ability. If we stumble and do something unholy, we may think we deserve punishment, but in reality Jesus bore our sins once for all at the Cross!

Balance: Humility

Both pride and condemnation stem from a mentality that is full of oneself. Humility dares to acknowledge that we can't do it on our own. James 4:10 says, *"Humble yourselves in the sight of the Lord, and He will lift you up."* What does humility look like? It looks like knowing who He is, bowing before Him in reverence, and allowing Him to lift you up into who He made you to be! Put your confidence in Him. Don't find your worth apart from what He has done, and you will always stay balanced. If salvation was the greatest gift, what makes us think that anything else in the Kingdom can be earned or worked for? This is something we can ponder to align our hearts with humility.

Application: The key to humility is to be consumed with a reverence for God and to be in awe of His love. Thankfulness will eradicate self-conceit. Write down five things you're grateful for and declare them until you become conscious of His goodness with a heart full of gratitude.

"True humility is not thinking less of yourself;
it is thinking of yourself less."
—C.S. Lewis

Day 23

Gifts of Impartation vs. Believing the Finished Work

Gifts of Impartation

1. **Origin:** *"Do not neglect the gift you have, which was given you by prophecy when the council of elders laid their hands on you." (1 Tim. 4:14)*

2. **Heartbeat:** God has given us many gifts! At the same time, He has surrounded us with people who have gifts that we have not yet started walking in. When we receive impartation, we are enabled to walk in the same anointings and giftings of those around us.

3. **Extreme—FOCUSED ON THE MAN OF GOD:** When we overemphasize impartation, people become our source of gifting and anointing. We cannot rely on people to receive things that only God can give. It's possible for us to become so focused on the man of God with the anointing that we actually forget about the God of man who gives the anointing to begin with.

Believing the Finished Work

1. **Origin:** *"As His divine power has given to us all things that pertain to life and godliness, through the knowledge of Him who called us by glory and virtue." (2 Pet. 1:3)*

2. **Heartbeat:** At the heart of Christianity is receiving what Christ has already done. We know that, because of His love, we are fully satisfied and complete.

3. **Extreme—SELF-SUFFICIENT PRIDE:** If we start taking this truth too far, we start thinking that because Jesus has given us

everything, we no longer need anyone else in our lives to impart to us or teach us anything. We become self-sufficient and prideful.

Balance: Honor

2 Timothy 1:6 says, *"Therefore I remind you to stir up the gift of God which is in you through the laying on of my hands."* After reading this passage, it's important to see that the laying on of hands stirs up the gift that is already inside of us. Christ has done everything on the Cross and we have every gift deposited within us. However, there is a truth to honoring leaders and allowing them to stir up the gifts that we possess. Anointing and covering flows through honor. Impartation is a beautiful display of freely giving away things that were freely given to us. It is valuable and beneficial, however we shouldn't be discouraged if someone important in a meeting doesn't feel led to lay their hands on us. Whether it be through a minister's impartation or a moment in the secret place, God will supply you with all you need for every circumstance.

Application: If you're someone who's never really thought much about receiving impartation, we encourage you to pray about it and see if there's someone the Lord wants to use to bless you. If impartation is normal for you, take some time to thank the Lord for all He's already deposited within you.

"To harmonize the thoughts and imaginations of men, the presence of the stimulating breath of the Holy Spirit is necessary. When that is present there will be produced heavenly airs and joyous harmonies in men's hearts, both in this life and in heaven."
—Sadhu Sundar Singh

Day 24

Honoring Men vs. Honoring God

Honoring Men

1. **Origin:** *"Be kindly affectionate to one another with brotherly love, in honor giving preference to one another." (Rom. 12:10)*
2. **Heartbeat:** We desire to do everything unto God and we know that serving people is a sign of walking selflessly and following Christ. We want to follow Christ's commands to love others and listen to what others have to say.
3. **Extreme—FEAR OF MAN:** We can take honor and loving others to an extreme when we become afraid of what people think or even could say to us. We think that being accepted by men is somehow equivalent to being loved by God, and we can begin to live by the ups and downs of what people think.

Honoring God

1. **Origin:** *"The fear of man brings a snare, but whoever trusts in the Lord shall be safe." (Prov. 29:25)*
2. **Heartbeat:** Having a desire to value the Word and trust in God, we put His voice first in our lives. We understand that it is He who saves us, brings freedom to us, and ultimately transforms us.
3. **Extreme—DISREGARDING MENS' COUNSEL:** We can take our interpretation of what God is speaking to us to the extreme when we don't recognize that God has put leaders and friends in our lives to help guide us. We think that men have nothing to add, which can result in ruined relationships and living in deception.

Balance: Reverent Fear of God

The balance between having the fear of man and completely disregarding the opinions of others is found in having a humble, reverent fear toward God. When we understand that God has placed relationships in our lives to help guide us, we will add weight to those relationships. However, we shouldn't let these relationships make or break us, as our identity needs to be centered on the Cross and everything He has done for us. It is by living in reverence and awareness of His selfless acts that we live a rich life. Proverbs 22:4 says, *"The reward of humility and the fear of the LORD are riches, honor and life."*

Application: Do you have friends in your life that are able to speak into different situations that you are going through? At the same time, do you feel yourself overcome by fear, anxiety, or lack of self-worth when you are around certain people? Take a step back, evaluate your life and ask God to show you His truth in the relationships you have built or maybe even avoided. Ask Him what relationships He has placed in your life, what their purpose is, and then make it a goal to pursue that person (those people) with the intention to hear God through them. *"If someone says, 'I love God,' and hates his brother, he is a liar; for he who does not love his brother whom he has seen, how can he love God whom he has not seen?"* (1 Jn. 4:20).

"Where there is fear of God to keep the house,
the enemy can find no way to enter."
—St. Francis of Assisi

Day 25

Creating Healthy Boundaries vs. Reckless Love

Creating Healthy Boundaries

1. **Origin:** *"And He said to them, 'Come away by yourselves to a secluded place and rest a while.'" (Mark 6:31 NASB)*

2. **Heartbeat:** We believe that it is impossible to single handedly meet the needs of every individual in ministry and we can't take on a false sense of responsibility for others. God calls us to define healthy boundaries that enable us to to love people well and cultivate prosperous relationships.

3. **Extreme—SELF-PRESERVATION:** We fall into the extreme when we reject someone in genuine need in the name of "setting healthy boundaries." We create a law to live by instead of living from a place of grace and compassion. We set ourselves safely in our own little box of comfort.

Reckless Love

1. **Origin:** *"Greater love has no one than this, that one lay down his life for his friends." (John 15:13)*

2. **Heartbeat:** Our great heart of compassion for the lost, broken, and needy fuels us to minister and take on some responsibility for those we encounter on a daily basis.

3. **Extreme—NO REST AND BURN OUT:** We slip into this extreme when we see ourselves as responsible for meeting all of the needs of those we serve in a twenty-four hour, seven day-a-week fashion. This will leave us exhausted and possibly feeling condemned about all those we cannot help.

Balance: Yielded to Grace

God calls us to set limits that protect ourselves from being ruled and overwhelmed by the demands of others. On the other hand, we need to make certain that those very limits do not ignore the needs or hurts of others. Jesus is a perfect example of how we can do this well. In Mark 6:31, we see him retreating to be with the Father, but in the next moment, we see him attending and miraculously feeding a crowd of five thousand people. In this context, living from grace looks like finding a place where we can be fully who we are, do what God has asked of us, and be sensitive to the needs of others. We are only able to live for something outside of ourselves when we yield and surrender to God and let His love overtake us.

Application: Yield to His grace today! Take twofold action: 1) Spend some time alone with the Lord Put your phone on silent and simply be with Him. 2) Make it your goal to do one inconvenient thing for another person today! (This could look like helping someone carry their groceries or even buying someone's coffee in line.)

"Don't waste your time consuming what makes you weak.
Spend your time pressing in for the Presence.
Become so intimate with Jesus, so full of Him, that it does not matter
what challenges in life present themselves to you.
You will be so spiritually full that you can feed a multitude of other
people's needs. Jesus will give you more than enough."
—Heidi Baker

Day 26

Meditation vs. Declaration

Meditation

1. **Origin:** *"But the Lord is in his holy temple: let all the earth keep silence before him." (Hab. 2:20)*
2. **Heartbeat:** It is extremely powerful to be still and know that He is God. God is holy and is worthy of our silent adoration. Meditating on His Word day and night is an act of communion that is intimate and empowering.
3. **Extreme—INEFFECTIVE WITNESS:** There is a lot of fruit that can come from meditation but we must not forget that there is power in our words. If the truth only remains a whisper in our hearts then it won't be able to help those around us. It can be unprofitable and potentially dangerous to remain quiet in a world crying for answers.

Declaration

1. **Origin:** *"The tongue has the power of life and death." (Prov. 18:21)*
2. **Heartbeat:** It is exciting to know how powerful our words are. They can move mountains in our lives and the lives of others. It was with words that creation came into being (see Heb. 11:3).
3. **Extreme—DISCONNECTED FROM HIS VOICE:** If all we do is speak and never take time to listen to His still, small voice, we will become dependent on our own declarations to keep our fire burning. If our hearts aren't getting filled with His whisper, we will never have anything of genuine worth to share from the rooftops (see Matt.10:27).

Balance: A Time to Speak, A Time to Listen

Ecclesiastes 3:7 says that there is *"a time to be silent and a time to speak."* Many times in our relationship with God we swing to one side or the other. We will either always meditate, but rarely put truth on our lips, or always declare, but never take time to restfully listen. When we see that in our communion with God there is a time for both, it frees us from being imprisoned to one side or the other. God loves to spend time with us. Whether we speak His name or think His name, He is in a good mood! We must not fear that our spiritual growth will be impeded should we major on one and not the other. After all, it takes both our heart *and* our mouth to experience God's salvation and righteousness (see Rom. 10:10).

Application: How do you approach God: in silence, or with verbal declarations? We challenge you to take the limits off. If you find yourself very quiet before God, take some time to proclaim the truth over your life. If you find yourself very vocal with Him, be still and simply listen for a portion of time. Remember this simple phrase: *When you hear Him, you can declare Him.*

"I will conclude with that excellent saying of Bernard: 'Lord, I will never come away from Thee without Thee.' Let this be a Christian's resolution, not to leave off his meditations of God till he find something of God in him."
—Thomas Watson

Day 27

Intercession vs. Taking Action

Intercession

1. **Origin:** *"The effective, fervent prayer of a righteous man avails much."* (Jas. 5:16)

2. **Heartbeat:** Prayer is powerful. When we pray in faith, we can expect amazing things to happen. Intercession is a way of leaning on the power of God, and not our own strength, to see a healthy desire come to pass.

3. **Extreme—PASSIVITY AND INACTION:** When prayer takes the place of necessary, practical action, we've stepped into error. We can actually allow fear and/or apathy to mask themselves as a "time of prayer". For example, if we spend all our time interceding for the lost, but never take the time to share Jesus with them, we've only fulfilled a portion of what we're called to do (see Mark 16:15-18).

Taking Action

1. **Origin:** *"Go therefore and make disciples of all the nations, baptizing them in the name of the Father and the Son and the Holy Spirit."* (Matt. 28:19)

2. **Heartbeat:** When we read the Great Commission, our hearts are set ablaze to go and tell. We are filled with the confidence that we have the answer the world is looking for.

3. **Extreme—SELF-RELIANT:** If we are constantly taking action to go and tell, we will forget a very important ingredient: prayer. It's dangerous when we begin to put the burden to help others on ourselves and forget to cast our cares on the Lord. If we are

running around trying to fix every situation in our own strength, we will grow weary and won't see the fruit we desire.

Balance: Pray and Go

"Even so faith, if it has no works, is dead, being by itself" (Jas. 2:17 *NASB*). We are called to pray and we are called to go. We cannot do one and neglect the other. When we pray in faith, we must live accordingly, anticipating our prayers' fulfillment. If we truly desire to see our co-workers transformed, our siblings saved, and our world changed, we need to water with our actions what we've planted with our prayers. It's also important to note that some circumstances don't need our action, just our prayers. In the same way, there are some circumstances that absolutely require us to act. We need the Lord's wisdom and guidance to know our role in each situation. However, if what we are praying for can be bettered with our actions, we can't allow fear or complacency to hinder our involvement.

Application: Spend some time in prayer. Pray for family, friends, current events, or anything else laid on your heart. Then, think over what you've prayed into. What actions do you feel the Lord is calling you to do so you can partner with Him in seeing your prayers come to pass?

"Praying for God to work is fine, but praying for Him to do what we should be doing is pointless."
—*Reinhard Bonnke*

Day 28

Healthy Emotions vs. Denying the Flesh

Healthy Emotions

1. **Origin:** *"And when Jesus went out He saw a great multitude; and He was moved with compassion for them, and healed their sick." (Matt. 14:14)*

2. **Heartbeat:** God has created us with emotions for a reason. It is with our senses that we can experience and express God in amazing ways. Having feelings is part of being made in the image of God.

3. **Extreme—LIVING BY FEELINGS:** When we start living by our feelings, we are treading into territory which was never supposed to influence us. If our emotions become the determining factor as to whether we will respond to the voice of the Holy Spirit, we have started living based on feelings instead of living by faith.

Denying the Flesh

1. **Origin:** *"Then Jesus said to His disciples, "If anyone desires to come after Me, let him deny himself, and take up his cross, and follow Me." (Matt. 16:24)*

2. **Heartbeat:** We are called to live as Jesus lived, not as the world says we are supposed to live. Therefore, we are not supposed to be controlled by our feelings but rather be led by Jesus into all truth.

3. **Extreme—LIVING IN DENIAL:** When we detach ourselves from all our emotions, senses, and feelings in order to religiously follow Jesus, we have stepped into denial. Emotions are real and

there are reasons why we feel the way we do. It's important that we discuss with the Lord the different emotions we experience, especially if we think He's speaking to us through them.

Balance: Faith

Romans 4:19-21 says, *"And not being weak in faith, he did not consider his own body, already dead (since he was about a hundred years old), and the deadness of Sarah's womb. He did not waver at the promise of God through unbelief, but was strengthened in faith, giving glory to God, and being fully convinced that what He had promised He was also able to perform."* Faith is the key to living in balance. If we live by faith, we are connected to the heart of Jesus, where all our emotions are supposed to be rooted. We are able to take the reality of a situation into account and then choose whether or not to act on what we are feeling. If we live in faith, we see what God is saying instead of what we are feeling or what we want to deny.

Application: When faced with a tough situation, ask yourself: "If Jesus was in this situation, how would He have handled it?" After envisioning how Jesus would act, do the same as He would have done, instead of reacting to your feelings or denying them altogether. Let faith become what you live by instead of what you feel or see happening in a situation.

"You should not believe your conscience and your feelings more than the word which the Lord who receives sinners preaches to you."
—Martin Luther

Day 29

Financial Wisdom vs. Radical Generosity

Financial Wisdom

1. **Origin:** *"But if anyone does not provide for his own, and especially for those of his household, he has denied the faith and is worse than an unbeliever." (1 Tim. 5:8 NASB)*

2. **Heartbeat:** We know that God has called us to be wise stewards of what's been given to us. It's important that we are able to provide for those we care for. We see that living in lack and need doesn't show the abundance Jesus paid for on the Cross.

3. **Extreme—SELFISH GAIN:** We can take this to the extreme by thinking that money's main purpose is to make our lives better. When we do this, we will always be looking for ways to save and protect our money. This may lead us to being overcome with anxiety and fear in times of financial uncertainty.

Radical Generosity

1. **Origin:** *"Sell your possessions and give to charity; make yourselves money belts which do not wear out, an unfailing treasure in heaven, where no thief comes near nor moth destroys. For where your treasure is, there your heart will be also." (Luke 12:33-34 NASB)*

2. **Heartbeat:** We have a heart to give to those around us and we constantly look for ways to sow into others' lives. We don't just give money, but we give our time, energy, and mental focus to help others succeed and grow.

3. **Extreme—INTENTIONAL POVERTY:** We can go too far if we find ourselves not being able to provide for the needs of our family

and personal life. We can start believing that God doesn't want us to have anything in this present life and we may even start to despise those who have wealth.

Balance: Stewardship

"The silver is Mine, and the gold is Mine,' says the Lord of hosts" (Hag. 2:8). The balance to both of these truths is found in recognizing that God has ultimately given us everything we have. We are called to steward what we have and to be resources for the Kingdom as we are led. Being a resource looks like giving and using what we have to produce more resources to pour into others. When we know that the things we own aren't truly ours, it is easy to give to those who are in need. All the while, we can trust that God will provide for our own needs because He cares for us! It's not about giving everything or keeping everything; it's about stewarding well what we've been given. We need to simply ask the Lord what He would have us do with what we possess and follow His leading.

Application: Take a notebook and set apart time with God to ask Him what resources He has given you, whether it be financial, physical, or relational. Take that list and seek Him for how to best steward those resources. How can you best invest your money? How can you best invest in the relationships you have? How can you best use your energy to serve others?

"The world asks, 'What does a man own?'
Christ asks, 'How does he use it?'"
—Andrew Murray

Day 30

God Meets My Needs vs. People Meet My Needs

God Meets My Needs

1. **Origin:** *"And my God shall supply all your need according to His riches in glory by Christ Jesus." (Phil. 4:19 NASB)*
2. **Heartbeat:** God is a good Father. He wants to supply us with everything we need for our enjoyment. He is all-sufficient and the source of all life.
3. **Extreme—ISOLATION:** We take this reality to the extreme when we deny help from the Body of Christ in times of need. This can leave us very isolated if we continually refuse to receive from those around us.

People Meet My Needs

1. **Origin:** *"And the eye cannot say to the hand, 'I have no need of you'; nor again the head to the feet, 'I have no need of you.'" (1 Cor. 12:21 NASB)*
2. **Heartbeat:** God created us to be relational beings, and throughout the New Testament we are constantly referred to as the Body of Christ. We also see God throughout the entire Bible celebrating unions between man and woman and blessing fathers, mothers, and children. We truly are created to walk with one another.
3. **Extreme—PEOPLE ARE MY SOURCE OF GRATIFICATION:** We have drifted into an unhealthy extreme if we focus on what people are or aren't doing for us rather than being in the relationship for selfless love. We can find ourselves seeking fulfillment and satisfaction from people rather than from God.

Balance: God Fulfills Us and Uses Others to Help

We may never have known that God loved us if we hadn't first seen it modeled by someone else. We may never have known that we were valuable to God if there wasn't another person there to show us. These acts from people are meant to be a revelation of God to us. Once the Person of Jesus has been revealed to us and we understand the Gospel, we will then see that we have free access to His love all the time. We will be positioned to freely give His love to those around us. It isn't wrong to be built up by others, but let us never forget that God is our true source of life, peace, grace, and affirmation, and that He alone should define our value.

Application: How do you view the people in your life? Do you feel that they are here simply for your betterment or that you are here to love them? God, by His grace, wants to empower you to be a walking encounter of His love everywhere you go. Take some time today to open your heart to Jesus and be affirmed by His Word. As you find yourself more aware of Him and His love, simply take it to the world around you. You truly are part of His Body here on Earth.

"Christ has no body but yours. No hands, no feet on earth but yours. Yours are the eyes with which He looks compassion on this world. Yours are the feet with which He walks to do good. Yours are the hands, with which He blesses all the world."
—Saint Teresa of Avila

Day 31

Church-Oriented vs. Evangelism-Oriented

Church-Oriented

1. **Origin:** *"They were continually devoting themselves to the apostles' teaching and to fellowship, to the breaking of bread and to prayer." (Acts 2:42 NASB)*

2. **Heartbeat:** It is our job as believers to get the Bride of Christ ready for the coming of the Bridegroom. Coming together as believers and building each other up in Christ causes development and growth in a congregation as well as in an individual.

3. **Extreme—EXCLUSIVITY:** If we become so consumed with what's going on inside of the four walls of the church, without seeing the bigger picture, we take the path of stagnation and exclusivity. The Church should not be so occupied with herself that she forgets the vital role she plays in the proclamation of hope to the lost.

Evangelism-Oriented

1. **Origin:** *"And He said to them, "Go into all the world and preach the gospel to all creation.""* (Mark 16:15)

2. **Heartbeat:** Jesus gave His followers the Great Commission to go and spread the Gospel into all the world. The primary way unbelievers experience salvation is through Christians exposing the Gospel to them.

3. **Extreme—UNDEVELOPED CHURCH:** There is an issue if we become so focused on our passion for evangelism that we start to neglect the importance of building up the Bride of Christ.

Going after seeing lost souls saved and spreading the Gospel without investing into our fellow brothers and sisters can lead to disunity. This will result in a Bride that is born again but still hurting.

Balance: Equip and Send

Ephesians 4:11-13 (NASB) says, *"And He gave some as apostles, and some as prophets, and some as evangelists, and some as pastors and teachers, for the equipping of the saints...until we all attain to the unity of the faith, and of the knowledge of the Son of God, to a mature man, to the measure of the stature which belongs to the fullness of Christ."* The Church is a flourishing place of vibrant unity and diversity, where the focus is on equipping the saints and making disciples so they will go out and change the world. We don't have to fixate solely on being evangelistic or pastoral. It's important that we value both in order to grow and increase the Church.

Application: If you find yourself in one of these extremes, step out in both building church community and also reaching out to non-believers. Start investing in small groups and home groups to build community within the Church and look for opportunities to demonstrate God's love to others outside the Church in everyday life.

"The Church exists for nothing else but to draw men into Christ, to make them little Christs. If they are not doing that, all the cathedrals, clergy, missions, sermons, even the Bible itself, are simply a waste of time. God became Man for no other purpose."
—C.S. Lewis

Day 32

God Loves the World vs. God Loves Me

God Loves the World

1. **Origin:** *"For God so loved the world that He gave His only begotten Son, that whoever believes in Him should not perish but have everlasting life." (John 3:16)*

2. **Heartbeat:** God loves the world. He did not come to condemn the world, but to save it (see John 3:17). We have a mandate to preach the Gospel and to co-labor with Heaven to rescue captives from the domain of darkness. Jesus did not distance Himself from the sinners and mess-ups, but broke bread with them and loved them.

3. **Extreme—IMPERSONAL CONNECTION WITH GOD:** When we become so focused on God's love for the world that we cannot see or appreciate His love for us as individuals, we have crossed into an extreme. When we live from this perspective, investing time into yourself or your private time with the Lord becomes tedious. We lose touch with that personal connection to Christ that matters more than anything.

God Loves Me

1. **Origin:** *"How precious to me are your thoughts, O God! How vast is the sum of them! If I would count them, they are more than the sand." (Ps. 139:17-18 NASB)*

2. **Heartbeat:** God desires to have an intimate relationship with us. He knows the number of hairs on our heads. God loves us as unique individuals and He desires to be intimate with us individually.

3. **Extreme—SELF-ABSORPTION:** Being unbalanced by focusing on God's love for you with no thought of the world around you leaves you self-absorbed and devoid of sympathy for others. This will ultimately undermine the urgency of the Gospel to reach the lost and unsaved.

Balance: God Loves Everyone

1 John 4:10, 19 (ESV) says, *"In this is love, not that we have loved God but that he loved us and sent his Son to be the propitiation for our sins... We love because he first loved us."* We can only love because He first loved us. God loves and cares for the world, but He made us individually as unique targets of His vast affection. We should live from a revelation of our value and worth. When we truly understand the value He places on us, we will see the value in others and reveal it to them.

Application: How do you perceive the love of God? Is it easier for you to focus on His love for the world or for you personally? Ask the Lord to deepen your love for the lost today and cause you to be bold in your witness. Ask Him also to reveal His love to you in a new and deeper way. Ask Him, *"God, what do you love about me? What do you love about the people around me?"*

"Saving us is the greatest and most concrete demonstration of God's love, the definitive display of His grace throughout time and eternity."
—David Jeremiah

Day 33

Having Peace with All Men vs. Having Sound Doctrine

Having Peace with All Men

1. **Origin:** *"If it is possible, as much as depends on you, live peaceably with all men." (Rom. 12:18)*

2. **Heartbeat:** Out of a desire to keep the peace, we position ourselves to receive from those around us, even those we disagree with. We take measures to submit our own way of thinking to those wiser than us in order to take on an entirely new way of thinking.

3. **Extreme—PASSIVE AGREEMENT WITH EVERYTHING:** We take this too far when we are afraid to speak and avoid disagreement with a leader or fellow believer. We may even begin to believe the lie that, if someone is leading us, then they have everything correct and have no need for help. In our minds, disagreeing means that we are dishonoring our leader or fellow believer and that we will ultimately be disconnected from them.

Having Sound Doctrine

1. **Origin:** *"He must hold firmly to the trustworthy word [of God] as it was taught to him, so that he will be able both to give accurate instruction in sound [reliable, error-free] doctrine and to refute those who contradict [it by explaining their error]." (Tit. 1:9 AMP)*

2. **Heartbeat:** We desire to create an environment around us that promotes sound doctrine, so we begin to take everything we have been taught and test it against the Word of God.

3. **Extreme—NARROW-MINDEDNESS:** This goes too far when we shift our focus from loving first to seeking only "right" and "wrong" theology. We end up listening constantly for what we agree and disagree with and, ultimately, we build walls and gather only with those that we agree with completely.

Balance: Honor and Family

Just like our earthly families, as we gather together as the Family of God, disagreements will happen! Having a disagreement is not indicative of a problem. In fact, in Acts we a see a disagreement within the Church at the Council at Jerusalem (see Acts 15). It is all about how we handle the disagreement. To disagree well, we need to remain humble by honestly seeking the truth on a matter, not desiring to be right or to prove others wrong. Pride oftentimes is what turns a disagreement into a quarrel. When questioning a leader, it is key to be humble and bring questions rather than cutting quotes from Scripture.

Application: Next time you disagree with a message you hear preached or have a disagreement with a fellow believer, develop a question that displays your interpretation of the issue and also seeks to know the heart of the person you are disagreeing with. Example: "I heard you say that _____. Help me understand where you are coming from, because when I read (this Scripture) I interpret it this way:_____."

"If you have learned how to disagree without being disagreeable, then you have discovered the secret of getting along."
—Bernard Meltzer

Day 34

Confidence vs. Meekness

Confidence

1. **Origin:** *"I can do all things through Him who strengthens me."* *(Phil. 4:13 NASB)*
2. **Heartbeat:** God has blessed us all with a myriad of unique gifts and abilities. We are made to excel in life with our God-given talents.
3. **Extreme—SELF-CONFIDENT/RELIANT:** We may begin to rely upon our own ability above God's if we grow impatient with His plan or uncertain with what He's doing. We begin to use our talents as leverage in life and forget that God has supplied us with these very abilities we are using to make a name for ourselves.

Meekness

1. **Origin:** *"My grace is sufficient for you, for power is perfected in weakness. Most gladly, therefore, I will rather boast about my weaknesses, so that the power of Christ may dwell in me." (2 Cor. 12:9 NASB)*
2. **Heartbeat:** We genuinely believe that we are nothing apart from God and that we are fully dependent and reliant upon Him. In meekness, we yield to His hand upon our lives.
3. **Extreme—INADEQUACY:** Oftentimes, we get too focused on our weaknesses instead of the empowerment of God which is available to all who believe. Those of us who don't know what the Cross accomplished will experience a constant sense of inadequacy.

Balance: God-Confidence

2 Corinthians 3:5 (NASB) says, *"Not that we are adequate in ourselves to consider anything as coming from ourselves, but our adequacy is from God."* If you lack confidence or find yourself relying upon your natural abilities, it's time to start finding your security in God. Self-confidence says that you are enough on your own whereas inadequacy and lack of confidence says that you are never enough. True confidence comes when your heart posture is one of trust and constantly abiding in God's love and acceptance. It takes faith to put your trust in someone outside of yourself. Confidence rooted in truth and humility is unshakeable. You can have the worst day yet know that your confidence is not found in what you do or don't do; it's found in who you are in Christ.

Application: Focus on God's ability in you today. Recognize that your confidence should not be rooted in what you do, but rather in what He has already done. We know that He will always come through and that His grace empowers us to do the impossible. If you are feeling weak, learn to lean on Him and find your confidence in Him. If you have victories in your life, give Him the praise because every win is truly a loss without Him. Focus on thankfulness and you will start to see a deep-rooted confidence develop in your life.

"Insecurity is wrong-placed security."
—Bill Johnson

Day 35

Spirit-Led Evangelism vs. Talking to Everyone

Spirit-Led Evangelism

1. **Origin:** *"For all who are led by the Spirit of God are sons of God."* *(Rom. 8:14 ESV)*
2. **Heartbeat:** As sons and daughters of God, we have the incredible opportunity and ability to hear the voice of God and to be led by the Spirit. As we grow in hearing His voice, He will lead us into specific situations where we can minister to people.
3. **Extreme—HOLDING BACK IN FEAR:** When we create an excuse to not speak to people because we feel like we weren't led by the Holy Spirit, we have started misusing this truth. We have taken this truth and started using it as a "spiritual crutch." We may find ourselves hiding behind the language of being "Spirit-led" as an alibi for fear.

Talking to Everyone

1. **Origin:** *"God anointed Jesus of Nazareth with the Holy Spirit and with power, who went about doing good and healing all who were oppressed by the devil, for God was with Him."* *(Acts 10:38)*
2. **Heartbeat:** Jesus healed everyone that He prayed for and we are called to live as He lived. Therefore, we should always be developing the Kingdom by seeing people saved and healed.
3. **Extreme—SELF-EFFORT EVANGELISM:** If we get so focused on talking to people and evangelizing, we may forget that it's the Spirit who does the work and that apart from Him, it's all pointless. We have prioritized our agenda above the voice and leading of the Holy Spirit.

Balance: Compelled by Love

1 Corinthians 13:1 says, *"Though I speak with the tongues of men and of angels, but have not love, I have become sounding brass or a clanging cymbal."* The Word says that God is love. Therefore, to live the way Jesus lived, we must have to be compelled by that same identity. We are to be known for our love. When we evangelize, we should constantly focus on the person of Jesus. We should recognize who He is pointing out to us, but we should also leave room to talk to people even if we don't necessarily feel the leading of the Spirit. When love is the motivator of what we do, we start seeing people through the eyes of love and we live with Heaven's agenda.

Application: Take time today to read 1 Corinthians 13, but instead of reading the word "love" insert "I" where "love" would be. For example, when reading "Love is patient, love is kind," you would read: "I am patient, I am kind." Be expectant to start living the way Jesus (Love) would live! Let the truth of what Jesus has done saturate your mind and cause you to be transformed!

"The best use of time is love. The best expression of love is time. The best time to love is now!"
—Rick Warren

Day 36

Pursuing More vs. Living in Rest

Pursuing More

1. **Origin:** *"I press on toward the goal for the prize of the upward call of God in Christ Jesus." (Phil. 3:14 NASB)*

2. **Heartbeat:** When we look at our lives, we see that everything is not yet perfected and polished. We have not yet attained all God has called us to. Therefore, we press on to bring ourselves closer to the standard that Jesus displayed for us.

3. **Extreme—STRIVING IN THE FLESH:** Our pursuit for more becomes extreme when we place no trust in God to bring about transformation in our lives, and we look to our own efforts for spiritual growth. This ultimately ends in misplaced faith (we trust our own ability beyond His) and the failure to experience His transformational power.

Living in Rest

1. **Origin:** *"For he who has entered His rest has himself also ceased from his works as God did from His." (Heb. 4:10)*

2. **Heartbeat:** Christ has ceased from His works, which means that we can cease from ours. His work of perfection is finished in us and there is nothing that we can add to it by our own efforts.

3. **Extreme—COMPLACENCY:** Our interpretation of this truth becomes extreme when we are tempted to ignore or deny areas of our lives where we have not yet seen transformation. We overlook behaviors that fall below Biblical standards, which leads to compromised character.

Balance: Grace-Powered Transformation

Transformation only works when its source is Jesus Christ. We are saved, not by merit of our righteousness, but according to His mercy (see Titus 3:5). When we take on the role of authoring our own transformation, we have taken Jesus off the throne and placed ourselves there instead. But to deny our need for transformation is to undermine the reason for the Cross entirely. Certainly, we do not yet see ourselves as we will be, but we can see the perfect example of Jesus Christ (see Heb 2:8-9). For that reason, we are to press on toward the upward call and take hold of the full measure of salvation Jesus has purchased for us!

Application: As you speak out these declarations, make the decision in your heart to step into balance and leave striving and complacency behind:

I am not the author of my own salvation!
I am pressing on toward the upward call of God in Christ Jesus!
I am made to look just like Him!

"Deny your weakness, and you will never realize
God's strength in you."
—Joni Eareckson Tada

Day 37

One Father vs. Many Teachers

One Father

1. **Origin:** *"For if you were to have countless tutors in Christ, yet you would not have many fathers, for in Christ Jesus I became your father through the gospel."* *(1 Cor. 4:15-16 NASB)*
2. **Heartbeat:** We should all desire to recognize a spiritual father/mother that God has placed in our life. We want a person who can speak into us from a holistic perspective and whom we can go to anytime to seek help.
3. **Extreme—CLOSE-MINDED:** We can take this truth to the extreme when we stop allowing other leaders besides our spiritual father/mother to impact us or give us wisdom. This can create tunnel vision and we won't be able to value other perspectives from people appointed by God to teach.

Many Teachers

1. **Origin:** *"Without counsel, plans go awry, But in the multitude of counselors they are established."* *(Prov. 15:22)*
2. **Heartbeat:** We recognize that there is a host of incredible influencers and speakers throughout the world and they all have unique insights to give us so, naturally, we want to listen to them! We desire to have counsel and wisdom from many people when we make decisions.
3. **Extreme—EASILY INFLUENCED BY MANY OPINIONS:** We move into the extreme of over-valuing many teachers when we don't submit ourselves under the leadership of a spiritual father/mother. This may lead to bouncing from one teaching or

leader to the next trying to seek the answer that we *want* to hear instead of staying with the answer we *need* to hear.

Balance: One Father, Many Teachers

"The things which you have heard from me in the presence of many witnesses, entrust these to faithful men who will be able to teach others also" (2 Tim. 2:2 NASB). We can see the balance in Paul's life by how he led those he was set over. He led them to the Lord and laid core foundations of truth in their life. He wasn't opposed to other teachers giving input and he even trained people to become teachers of what he had taught them. While it's important for us to have a spiritual father/mother who can disciple us, we should also be open to learn from different leaders who carry wisdom on various subjects.

Application: Ask God if there is a leader in your life that He desires for you to connect with on a deeper level. Take time to pursue that relationship and allow it to grow. At the same time, make it a goal to listen to one sermon a week that is outside of your church circle so that you can get insights you may not normally hear. Find books and use the relationship with the leader you are pursuing to find more influences to grow from.

"Cheap grace is grace without discipleship, grace without the cross, grace without Jesus Christ."
—Dietrich Bonhoeffer

Day 38

Radical Faith vs. Living in Wisdom

Radical Faith

1. **Origin:** *"He did not waver at the promise of God through unbelief, but was strengthened in faith, giving glory to God, and being fully convinced that what He had promised He was also able to perform."* *(Rom. 4:20-21)*

2. **Heartbeat:** Radical faith stems from a childlike zeal to do the works of the Lord, trusting that all things will work together for good. Faith convinces us of a reality beyond what we see.

3. **Extreme—IMPULSIVENESS:** We begin to live impulsively when we use our "faith" as an excuse to do reckless things (Ex: spending large amounts of money you don't have). However, these rash decisions are often zealous acts void of wisdom. Faith will have results. Human impulse will not.

Living in Wisdom

1. **Origin:** *"Therefore be careful how you walk, not as unwise men but as wise."* *(Eph. 5:15 NASB)*

2. **Heartbeat:** As Christians we desire to walk in wisdom. We don't want to walk through a situation without assessing and viewing it properly.

3. **Extreme—OVERLY CAUTIOUS:** Caution becomes a stumbling block when we cling to it in the name of wisdom, while in reality we are allowing fear to hold us back. Caution should never be used as an excuse to disobey the voice of the Lord.

Balance: God's Heavenly Wisdom

Wisdom and discernment are gifts from God. *"If any of you lacks wisdom, let him ask God, who gives generously to all without reproach, and it will be given him"* (James 1:5 ESV). God's perfect wisdom knows when to act radically and when to stay at rest. If we abide in God's wisdom, we will learn to discern the situations we face and how we should approach them. As we walk through life, we need to take time to discern His voice and to walk accordingly. We will be liberated from impulsiveness and compelled by love to kick our fears of caution in the face as we patiently wait to hear His voice.

Application: Pray the following prayer: *"Father, I thank you for sending Your one and only Son, Jesus! I thank you that through Christ I have been redeemed and adopted into Your family! I thank You that as your sheep, You have given me the ability to hear Your voice. Father, I ask that You would give me greater discernment and wisdom, so that I may live a balanced and truth-centered life that's free from fear and full of heavenly wisdom. Amen!"*

"We need discernment in what we see and what we hear and what we believe."
—Charles Swindoll

Day 39

Ambition vs. Contentment

Ambition

1. **Origin:** *"Fight the good fight of faith, lay hold on eternal life, to which you were also called and have confessed the good confession in the presence of many witnesses." (1 Tim. 6:12)*

2. **Heartbeat:** Each of us are called to do great and powerful things. A healthy ambition will drive us into growth and development and will prepare us for God's plans for our lives. It's important we don't settle for less when there is so much in store for us in Christ.

3. **Extreme—PERFORMANCE:** Ambition becomes unhealthy when we put high expectations on ourselves which were never a requirement from God or people to begin with. In that case, our ambition can make us impatient with the process and leave us performing for achievements in our own strength.

Contentment

1. **Origin:** *"Not that I speak in regard to need, for I have learned in whatever state I am, to be content." (Phil 4:11)*

2. **Heartbeat:** It's important to stay content amidst the various highs and lows of life. When we are rooted in Christ, we will find ourselves satisfied by Him through every situation we face.

3. **Extreme—LACK OF PASSION:** If we refrain from living a life of spiritual fervor and excellence because "we are content", we have swung to the extreme. Christ didn't come to make us comfortable in our little shells, He came to transform us so that we would, in turn, transform the world around us.

Balance: Christ Our Role Model

Ephesians 5:1-2 says, *"Therefore be imitators of God as dear children. And walk in love, as Christ also has loved us and given Himself for us, an offering and a sacrifice to God for a sweet-smelling aroma."* When you focus on becoming like Christ, the extremes fall to the wayside. Don't allow where you're *not* to stir up an unhealthy and reckless ambition that discounts the process. At the same time, don't allow where you *are* to shake your contentment and satisfaction in Christ. When you make it your goal to become like Jesus and to love like Him, all of the pieces will come together. No matter where you are or what you're doing, what truly makes life extraordinary is knowing God and displaying His image.

Application: What about you? Do you have a burning passion to change the world, but feel stuck in the mundane? Or do you find yourself simply "okay" with life and lacking motivation? In either case, lay it all down! Fix your eyes on Jesus and pray this prayer: *"Thank you Father that I was never made to live an ordinary life. Thank you that it's not about where I am, but about who I am. Father, make me shine like Your Son right here, right now. I know you are leading me into great and powerful things. I love you and I trust you. Amen!"*

"The more you pray, the more you are stating your desire to live your life by God's standards."
—Jim George

Day 40

God Is Sovereign vs. Free Will

God is Sovereign

1. **Origin:** *"Your eyes saw my substance, being yet unformed. And in Your book they all were written, the days fashioned for me, when as yet there were none of them." (Ps. 139:16)*

2. **Heartbeat:** When we realize that the entirety of our life was ordained by God before we were formed, a sense of calm and rest comes, knowing that He is in control. We don't need to worry about tomorrow because He is Lord.

3. **Extreme—APATHETIC AND UNINITIATED CHURCH:** In a pure heart of entering His rest, we can veer into the extreme when we stop taking responsibility for our actions and our lives and say, "God has predetermined that I would do what I did." When we fall into sin, someone we pray for doesn't get healed, or we pray and nothing changes, we then begin to believe that "whatever will be, will be" instead of realizing that our circumstances are not lining up with the truth of God's Word.

Free Will

1. **Origin:** *"I call heaven and earth as witnesses today against you, that I have set before you life and death, blessing and cursing; therefore choose life, that both you and your descendants may live." (Deut. 30:19)*

2. **Heartbeat:** We realize God placed the power of choice in our hands. What happens to us and through us depends on what we choose. Through this we see that, when there is a natural disaster or someone is sick, we have been given authority to see

the Kingdom manifest in the situation. This motivates us to bring the solution to the problems we see.

3. **Extreme—SELF-RELIANT CHURCH:** While we continue to choose the ways of God, we go to the extreme when we rely wholly upon our own choices to define what happens in and through us. This pushes out the influence of God in our circumstances because we believe that He does not intervene, but has rather left everything up to us.

Balance: Partnering with God

Jesus said that He came down not to do His own will, but to do the will of the One who sent Him (see John 6:38). Jesus had the choice to decide what He wanted to do, but in humility He submitted to what the Father had in store for Him. The choice is also ours to partner with and submit to the sovereign God. We must realize that everything starts with God. He is the ultimate initiator of all things; we love because He first loved us, we breathe because He first breathed into us. Our job is to find what He has put in motion and choose to partner with what He is doing.

Application: Take time to ask God the following questions and write down the answers: "Where are you leading me in my life? What is one thing you desire to do through me today? How can I partner with you in seeing that happen?"

"I used to ask God to help me. Then I asked if I might help Him. I ended up by asking God to do His work through me."
—Hudson Taylor

Day 41

Utilizing Ministry Tools vs. Relying on God's Voice

Utilizing Ministry Tools

1. **Origin:** *"And He Himself gave some...for the equipping of the saints for the work of ministry, for the edifying of the body of Christ." (Eph. 4:11-12)*

2. **Heartbeat:** The wide variety of teachings and tools offered by various ministries are here to equip the Body of Christ and bring her into her full identity and calling.

3. **Extreme—RELIANT ON MINISTRY TOOLS:** Most ministry methods are God-inspired and have proven effective. However, when we rely solely on a tool as our solution, the water gets murky. When tools don't work for us, we quickly start to question God's integrity. When we esteem ministry tools above our relationship with God, we have stepped out of line with His intent for us.

Relying on God's Voice

1. **Origin:** *"That we should no longer be children, tossed to and fro and carried about with every wind of doctrine, by the trickery of men, in the cunning craftiness of deceitful plotting." (Eph. 4:14)*

2. **Heartbeat:** Our earnest desire to never be carried away by strange teachings of men causes us to avoid unfamiliar teachings and methods of ministry, and we rely solely on our relationship with God through Scripture.

3. **Extreme—REJECTING MINISTRY TOOLS:** We might find that we become wary of ministry tools due to a previous bad experience or negative hearsay. That heart posture of distrust causes us to

rely only on what's been personally revealed to us. In the process, we discredit the tools that other ministries provide and the revelations that they walk in.

Balance: Christ-Centered

The balance is to be Christ-centered in all situations. When your attention is on the Eternal One, your life will take on a different dimension. Colossians 3:2-3 says, *"Set your mind on things above, not on things on the earth. For you died, and your life is hidden with Christ in God."* Your issues were buried with Christ and your life is found in Him. His resurrection power is flowing through your veins. When Christ is at the center of it all, we can trust Him to lead and guide us into freedom. We need to be attentive to His voice when it comes to ministry. It's not about pulling out your assortment of tools, it's about being led by Jesus and saying what He's saying. Tools have their place, but they must be God inspired!

Application: Do you find that you are constantly focused on fixing what is wrong with you? If so, we encourage you to ask God to illuminate Christ's victory to you. Meditate on the Cross and He will renew your mind to the truth. On the other hand, do you feel you have resentment toward ministry tools? In this case, ask a leader if there are any tips or tricks you can learn from them when it comes to ministering to people. And, if you are going through a struggle, ask them for advice on what to do!

"If your ministry can't work without you, then it is no longer Christ-centered. Minister toward Jesus, not yourself."
—Rev. Kellen Roggenbuck

Day 42

Deliverance Ministry vs. Already Delivered

Deliverance Ministry

1. **Origin:** *"For we do not wrestle against flesh and blood, but against principalities, against powers, against the rulers of the darkness of this age, against spiritual hosts of wickedness in the heavenly places." (Eph. 6:12)*

2. **Heartbeat:** We as believers are called to walk in the victory that Jesus paid for on the Cross. Part of this is casting out demons and interceding for others' breakthrough.

3. **Extreme—DEMON-HUNTING:** Taken too far, this truth can start giving us a very "devil-focused" view. We start seeing people through a tainted lens, and we focus more on the demonic influences on their life instead of seeing them how Jesus sees them.

Already Delivered

1. **Origin:** *"He has delivered us from the power of darkness and conveyed us into the kingdom of the Son of His love." (Col. 1:13)*

2. **Heartbeat:** God has done a powerful work for all of us through His Son. He has ultimately won and ultimately delivered every believer from the grips of darkness.

3. **Extreme—NO DELIVERANCE:** If we find ourselves avoiding the topic of demons altogether and pass off every issue as being "human nature", we have swung to an extreme. Demons have the ability to influence both believers and non-believers, therefore we cannot write off the fact that people do need freedom and deliverance (see 2 Cor. 11:3, Eph. 6:12).

Balance: Submit to God

Demons are real, but the Cross is a greater reality. In order to see God's reality of victory made manifest, it's important that we surrender our lives fully to God. James 4:7 says, *"Therefore submit to God. Resist the devil and he will flee from you."* Submission to God allows us to receive from God. He has victory over everything in this world and, when we submit our thoughts and our lives to Him, then we are able to resist the devil. John 8:32 says, *"And you shall know the truth, and the truth shall make you free."* The truth that we need to understand when casting out demons is that God has given us all authority. We simply need to believe it. We have to keep our focus on Jesus (submit to God) and remember what His grace empowers us to do (resist the devil). Then we will see the enemy flee.

Application: Start today by making this declaration out loud: *"My surrender to God gives me victory over the devil."* If you don't believe it the first time, declare it and keep on declaring it until this truth becomes a motto that you live by. When you say "yes" to God and give Him your all, then your whole being will be enraptured in His victory.

"What you believe is powerful. If you can change what you believe, you can change your life!"
—Joseph Prince

Day 43

Secular vs. Sacred

Secular

1. **Origin:** *"To the Jews I became as a Jew, that I might win Jews... to the weak I became as weak, that I might win the weak. I have become all things to all men, that I might by all means save some." (1 Cor. 9:22)*

2. **Heartbeat:** We believe that to see the world impacted we have to be relevant to those around us. We don't want to be unapproachable, but rather known as the most fun, loving, and joyful people to be around!

3. **Extreme—WORLDLY STANDARDS:** We cross the line when we start living exactly as the world lives and are no longer showing them who Jesus is by the way we live. We allow the people we were meant to influence to influence us if we settle and live at a lower standard than Jesus personally lived.

Sacred

1. **Origin:** *"But you are a chosen generation, a royal priesthood, a holy nation, His own special people, that you may proclaim the praises of Him who called you out of darkness into His marvelous light." (1 Pet. 2:9)*

2. **Heartbeat:** We are called to be God's possession. We no longer have the right to do many of the things that we did before we knew Him. We are called to live at a higher standard that reveals the nature of Jesus to the world.

3. **Extreme—JUDGMENT AND SEPARATION:** We've taken this truth too far when we avoid and disapprove of those who act in

opposition to our "holy view." We shouldn't use holiness as an excuse to stay away from certain people or activities.

Balance: Do All Unto the Lord

We are called to be the salt of the earth. If we really understood that concept, we would realize that our holiness should start affecting the people around us. 1 Peter 1:15-16 says, *"But as He who called you is holy, you also be holy in all your conduct, because it is written, 'Be holy, for I am holy.'"* It is clear that we are called to live a holy lifestyle no matter what we do. Whether we are the only Christian surrounded by many unsaved people at work or we are doing mundane tasks to serve in church, our thought should be, "I am doing this unto the Lord." Everything we do is to be done unto God. Holiness isn't restricted to religious duties; holiness can look like loving the lost or having fun with Jesus! What's important is allowing Jesus to have the greatest influence on your heart.

Application: As you go about your day, make it your goal to do everything unto the Lord. Pray before you go into work, the grocery store, a hangout, or a meeting and say, *"God, this is for you. It's all for You. Let this be worship in your sight."* When you do the mundane, everyday things, know that they can be done for the glory of God and it can show people around you what Jesus would do in that very moment!

"As we grow in the knowledge of God's holiness, even though we are growing in the practice of holiness, it seems the gap between our knowledge and our practice always gets wider. This is the Holy Spirit's way of drawing us to more and more holiness."
—Jerry Bridges

Day 44

Intellectual vs. Spiritual

Intellectual

1. **Origin:** *"Study and do your best to present yourself to God approved, a workman [tested by trial] who has no reason to be ashamed, accurately handling and skillfully teaching the word of truth." (2 Tim. 2:15 AMP)*

2. **Heartbeat:** As lovers of truth, we make it a goal to be able to rightly divide the Word of God. We use our intellect to explain the truth and logically explain what we believe.

3. **Extreme—REJECTING THE SPIRIT:** We err to the extreme when we deny the acts and truths of the Spirit that don't make sense to us. When God does something radical for someone, our minds cannot comprehend the irrationality of it and thereby reject it.

Spiritual

1. **Origin:** *"But the natural man does not receive the things of the Spirit of God, for they are foolishness to him; nor can he know them, because they are spiritually discerned." (1 Cor. 2:14)*

2. **Heartbeat:** We understand the importance of relying on the Holy Spirit alone to bring revelation about the things of God. This reality is solidified in us the more we experience it for ourselves.

3. **Extreme—REJECTING THE INTELLECT:** We get unbalanced when we believe that any knowledge acquired apart from an encounter with the Holy Spirit is inferior. This can lead us to over-spiritualizing things.

Balance: Christ Is All

The problem is the perceived sense of conflict between these two supposed opposites. When we understand that all wisdom is from God, what we call human knowledge/ intelligence would bring us toward a revelation of Him. Colossians 2:3 puts it well when it says that in *"Christ... are hidden all the treasures of wisdom and knowledge."* God is the inventor of all true knowledge; therefore we conclude that both intellectuality and spirituality are doors of exploration into what God has already set in motion: we have just categorized them into different subjects. That being said, any knowledge, doctrine, or experience that doesn't lead us to a deeper knowledge of Christ is vain and empty.

Application: Be slow to speak or criticize when it comes to varied doctrines, teachings, or differences in opinion, for judgement will not save anyone. Prioritize relationship above what you believe, for that is most valuable. Division within the Body of Christ is never God's desire. Whenever a conflict arises because of a difference in beliefs, consciously choose love. For a fun activity, research amazing scientific facts online. As you read them, focus your attention on the God who made it all happen. Let Him reveal His nature to you through the truths scientists are discovering.

"Every theology should lead to a doxology
[the worship of God]."
—Anonymous

Day 45

Working Hard vs. God Supplies My Needs

Working Hard

1. **Origin:** *"He who has a slack hand becomes poor, but the hand of the diligent makes rich."* (Prov. 10:4)
2. **Heartbeat:** It is beneficial to have a good work ethic that says, "In order to generate an income, I have to work hard for it." This not only teaches us discipline, but it also gives us a healthy value for money that will lead us to manage it well.
3. **Extreme—SERVING MAMMON:** We take this mindset to an extreme if we work so hard for finances that we become victims to money and let it rule over us. If we strive for money in an unhealthy way and become dependent on it, we can let money dictate our contentment rather than God and make the spirit of mammon a god in our lives.

God Supplies My Needs

1. **Origin:** *"But my God shall supply all your need according to his riches in glory by Christ Jesus."* (Phi. 4:19 KJV)
2. **Heartbeat:** We desire to put our whole trust in God and believe that He is a good Father, who cares for our every need. Only good things come from Him and He promised us that He is our Provider.
3. **Extreme-IDLENESS:** It is dangerous if we take our perception of grace too far and think that, because God provides, we don't have to work and can simply wait on Him to move. In order to experience God's provision, it's necessary that we partner with Him.

Balance: Trust

2 Corinthians 9:8 says, *"And God is able to make all grace abound toward you, that you, always having all sufficiency in all things, may have an abundance for every good work."* When we live in trust, we live in partnership with God. As we give Him something to work with, we can be still and have a confidence that He will provide no matter what. Grace does not exclude hard work, nor does it promote laziness. However, if we find ourselves restleslessly working for money, it may indicate that we've become a victim to our next paycheck. Jesus says His yoke is easy and His burden is light. When we trust Him, we should never get to a place of burn-out or hopelessness about anything.

Application: Examine your lifestyle. Do you think you have let money rule you? Are there areas in your life where you haven't trusted the Lord for His provision? Or have you used grace as an excuse to not put work or effort into something? If so, ask the Lord for forgiveness and ask Him to lead you into truth and show you an action plan of what a healthy, financial lifestyle looks like. Take notes of what He reveals to you.

"One of the dangers of having a lot of money is that you may be quite satisfied with the kinds of happiness money can give and so fail to realize your need for God. If everything seems to come simply by signing checks, you may forget that you are at every moment totally dependent on God."
—C.S. Lewis

Day 46

All Things Permissible vs. Not All Beneficial

All Things Permissible

1. **Origin:** *"All things are lawful for me, but not all things are helpful; all things are lawful for me, but not all things edify."* (1 Cor. 10:23)
2. **Heartbeat:** The Cross sets us free from the yoke of slavery we once lived in. We are no longer under the law of sin and death and we have the liberty to do what is right from our hearts.
3. **Extreme—INDULGENT AND SINFUL:** This can become a dangerous extreme if we embrace sin and use this Scripture to justify our behavior. (Example: Living in gluttony and eating as much cake as you want because, "all things are lawful.")

Not All Beneficial

1. **Origin:** *"All things are lawful for me, but not all things are helpful; all things are lawful for me, but not all things edify."* (1 Cor. 10:23)
2. **Heartbeat:** After reading that not all things edify, we abstain from worldly things in excess out of the desire to live holy, pure, and clean before the Lord.
3. **Extreme—FEARFUL AND OVERLY CAUTIOUS:** It can become unhealthy if our abstinence from things comes from fear. (Example: Not eating cake because you are afraid of the sugar, GMO's, and gluten.)

Balance: Following Your Awakened Conscience

The truth is that yes, all things are in fact lawful and permissible for me, but since Christ lives in me, I am no longer governed by the system that says, *"do not eat, do not touch"* (see Colossians 2:21). The prophet Isaiah spoke of the day when Christ would awaken our conscience when he said: *"And your ears SHALL HEAR A WORD..." (Isaiah 30:21 ESV)*. We are now in a relationship with Jesus where we are no longer governed by law, but by a redeemed conscience. I can eat cake if I want to without fear of what is in the ingredients because Jesus is not of this world, and He isn't affected by GMO's. But when I hear a voice say, "That's probably enough for now", I stop. The conscience is the voice we so often hear, but unfortunately so often ignore. It's the still, small voice that helps us discern what is right and wrong for us in the moment. It's no longer a law, but an internal conversation, that helps us make decisions. So we don't need to live in fear of what's right and wrong; we need only to live attentive to His voice and He will guide us into all truth!

Application: We believe the Lord desires to awaken every believer's conscience! As you finish this day's devotional, expect to hear God in a fresh way. Ask Him to awaken your conscience in any place where you are still living under the law, and ask Him for the grace to follow His voice in everything you do. Make today a day where you decide to honor His voice and direction above all else and follow Him.

"Conscience is a God-given current standard of holiness."
—Watchman Nee

Day 47

Being Respectful vs. Being Bold for God

Being Respectful

1. **Origin:** *"Honor all people. Love the brotherhood. Fear God. Honor the king." (1 Pet. 2:17 NASB)*

2. **Heartbeat:** Out of respect for people, we make it our goal to aim for peaceful relations. We don't want to make people uncomfortable, and we certainly don't want them to feel belittled. It's with a heart full of love that we desire to be respectful.

3. **Extreme—STAGNANCY:** If we want people to feel blessed and honored more than seeing them transformed, we've allowed our respect to fizzle into stagnancy. Respect and fear can look very similar on the outside.

Being Bold for God

1. **Origin:** *"Preach the word; be ready in season and out of season; reprove, rebuke, and exhort, with complete patience and teaching." (2 Tim. 4:2 ESV)*

2. **Heartbeat:** It's extremely vital to preach God's Word with great boldness. A healthy spiritual life is sprinkled with testimonies of taking risks for God in seemingly inopportune times.

3. **Extreme—BEING INCONSIDERATE:** If we never take people, our surroundings, or the law into account before doing something radical for God, we run the risk of doing more damage than good. It's not always the time or place to stand up and shout the Gospel.

Balance: Discerning How to Love

"And this I pray, that your love may abound still more and more in knowledge and all discernment, that you may approve the things that are excellent..." (Phil. 1:9-10). Love looks like something. However, it doesn't always express itself the same way. We need discernment from God's Spirit to truly know what love should look like in any given situation. Sometimes it may look like leaving the waiter a generous tip, and sometimes it may look like taking the waiter by the hand and praying for God's Spirit to touch him in power. If we are attentive to His voice, we will be liberated from both extremes. We won't merely live quiet, respectful lives of love, nor will we solely live outspoken lives of boldness where we preach in every store. We will live exciting, surrendered lives saturated with both.

Application: You are called to be a written epistle of Christ, seen and read by all men. Pray this prayer before you start your day: *"God, give me discernment to know how to love the people around me. I don't want to live in fear, nor do I want to push my own agenda on people. Teach me to love just like you would in every situation. Amen."*

"Love looks like something, yet it has no limits."
—Heidi Baker

Day 48

Pursuing Earthly Leaders vs. God Is My Leader

Pursuing Earthly Leaders

1. **Origin:** *"Where there is no counsel, the people fall; But in the multitude of counselors there is safety." (Prov. 11:14)*
2. **Heartbeat:** In order to be rich in wisdom, we may find ourselves seeking the counsel of many to help us grow and make the best possible decisions. There is wisdom in a multitude of counselors.
3. **Extreme—LACK OF CONNECTION WITH GOD:** While it is important to seek wisdom from leaders, we can't allow them to become our source rather than our connection to God. If we find ourselves constantly turning to people rather than to God, we have stepped into an extreme.

God Is My Leader

1. **Origin:** *"But the anointing which you have received from Him abides in you, and you do not need that anyone teach you; but as the same anointing teaches you concerning all things, and is true, and is not a lie, and just as it has taught you, you will abide in Him." (1 Jn. 2:27)*
2. **Heartbeat:** We honor the Lord as our ultimate leader. This rises from a heart that desires to walk as His sheep, hearing His voice (see John 10:27). It should be our aspiration to be completely dependent on Jesus and what He has for us.
3. **Extreme—ISOLATION FROM EARTHLY LEADERSHIP:** It is true that Jesus is our Teacher, as He holds all truth, knowledge, and understanding. However, we step outside of wisdom when we

begin to cut earthly leadership out of our lives because we already have a teacher/leader in Jesus.

Balance: God Establishes Authority

Romans 13:1 says, *"Let every soul be subject to the governing authorities. For there is no authority except from God, and the authorities that exist are appointed by God."* In order to live in proper alignment with God's Word we must remember that God is the true teacher, but He has also placed leaders over us that we can learn from. Paul said it like this, *"Imitate me, just as I also imitate Christ" (1 Cor. 11:1).* In other words, we follow our leaders in order to grow further into the image of Christ. Don't be afraid to hear from God on your own. At the same time, don't be afraid to bring what you've heard from Him to a leader for further advice.

Application: Jesus will always be our Teacher, so it is crucial that we make sure we are personally hearing the voice of the Lord. At the same time, it is important to remember that discipleship is a huge part of following Christ (see Matt. 28:18-20). We are to not only make disciples, but also be discipled. If you don't currently have anyone speaking into your life, write down a list of a few people you really admire and feel like you could learn from. Take steps toward connecting with those people. If you do have someone personally mentoring you, then take some time to thank them and ask God for an encouraging word for them!

"If we truly value His presence above all, we will recognize and celebrate His presence resting on another."
—Bill Johnson

Day 49

Stopping for the One vs. Focused on Task at Hand

Stopping for the One

1. **Origin:** *"Assuredly, I say to you, inasmuch as you did it to one of the least of these My brethren, you did it to Me."* (Matt. 25:40)
2. **Heartbeat:** It is so vital that we stop to love people in the midst of our busy days. People are worth our time! With tender hearts we are compelled to stop for the one.
3. **Extreme—DISTRACTED AND INEFFECTIVE:** Overusing the strength of stopping for the one will hinder us from accomplishing the current objective we've been given. We can't allow our fear of leaving a person untouched to keep us from doing what we've been called to do.

Focused on Task at Hand

1. **Origin:** *"But He answered and said, "I was not sent except to the lost sheep of the house of Israel. Then she came and worshiped Him, saying, 'Lord, help me!' But He answered and said, 'It is not good to take the children's bread and throw it to the little dogs.'"* (Matt. 15:24-26)
2. **Heartbeat:** Much like Jesus in the passage above, we all have specific objectives to fulfill. We are called to accomplish both small and great things. Diligent hearts desire to see their purpose and daily goals completed.
3. **Extreme—LACK OF COMPASSION:** If we are always looking at the big picture and never stop to love the one, then we've stepped into error. We all have things we need to get done, but if we read the verses directly following the passage given above,

we find that Jesus had compassion to bless those who weren't in His immediate course of direction.

Balance: See the Goal, Love the People

"The goal of our instruction is love..." (1 Tim. 1:5 NASB). In the midst of our everyday lives, as we go about our duties, we need to realize that our ultimate task and goal is to love like Jesus. We all know the story of the woman with the issue of blood. Jesus was actually focused on the task at hand in the moment: to go and heal Jairus' daughter. However, while on the way, the sick woman touched Jesus and was made whole. Jesus took the time to acknowledge her faith and bless her, and then proceeded to go and raise the man's daughter from the dead. We need to keep focused on the task at hand, but we also need to see that the people we run into on the way are valuable and precious to God, too.

Application: Make these declarations over your life before you take on the tasks of the day:
I am a responsible person who accomplishes their goals.
I am excited about the people I will run into today.
My ultimate objective today is to love.

"Love is the doorway through which the human soul passes from selfishness to service."
—Jack Hyles

Day 50

Accepting the Sinner vs. Protecting the Sheep

Accepting the Sinner

1. **Origin:** *"For God did not send the Son into the world to judge the world, but that the world might be saved through Him." (John 3:17 NASB)*

2. **Heartbeat:** Jesus came to love the world, not to condemn and reject it. We are called to do the same. With hearts full of compassion, we need to love even the most wretched and unlovable sinner.

3. **Extreme—CONDONING SIN:** There's a fine line between accepting the sinner and actually endorsing their error. While we do need to love the sinner like Christ does, we must not ignore the fact that they need salvation.

Protecting the Sheep

1. **Origin:** *"If anyone comes to you and does not bring this teaching, do not receive him into your house, and do not give him a greeting; for the one who gives him a greeting participates in his evil deeds." (2 Jn. 10-11 NASB)*

2. **Heartbeat:** We cannot allow the leaven of the enemy to influence our lives or the lives of those we love. With that in mind, it's not always wise to allow sinners into a place where they could have a potentially negative influence.

3. **Extreme—CONDEMNING SINNERS:** We go to the extreme when we stop loving those whose behavior may be detrimental to the cultural development of congregations/communities. Even if we let someone know that we don't want their sinful habits

affecting our "sheep," we shouldn't stop loving them. We should pray that God touches them. If we find ourselves always shutting out sinners, we've forgotten the Cross and are in error.

Balance: Unconditional Love

"And on some have compassion, making a distinction; but others save with fear, pulling them out of the fire, hating even the garment defiled by the flesh" (Jude 22-23). We are called to show mercy and to love even as Christ did. If we only see people for the sin they've committed then we aren't seeing through the eyes of God's Spirit.

We must see people as they are: worth the price of Jesus' own blood. If they are lost in sin, we must reject the sin, but deeply love the slave lost in its grip. We must face each situation with the lost in wisdom and attentiveness to God's voice; we want to know the best way to love people. We are called to lovingly accept people without endorsing their sinfulness. That's what Jesus did for each one of us. We must also see the value of loving those we are shepherding. Sometimes turning away a negative influence is what is ultimately best for your church, friends, or family.

Application: Meditate on this passage today and ask the Lord to transform the way you see people. *"For Christ's love compels us, because we are convinced that one died for all, and therefore all died... So from now on we regard no one from a worldly point of view. Though we once regarded Christ in this way, we do so no longer"* (2 Cor. 5:14, 16).

"God teaches us to love by putting some unlovely people around us. It takes no character to love people who are lovely and loving to you."
—Rick Warren

111

Day 51

Bearing One Another's Burdens vs. Empowering Others

Bearing One Another's Burdens

1. **Origin:** *"Bear one another's burdens, and thereby fulfill the law of Christ." (Gal. 6:2 NASB)*
2. **Heartbeat:** We are called to walk with compassion just as Christ did, looking to support and encourage those around us. Jesus knew that He had within Him the power to change the lives of the people that He came in contact with.
3. **Extreme—TAKING ON FALSE RESPONSIBILITY:** We have stepped into error when we start living solely to "rescue" the people around us. When the problems of others come before our time with God or family then we will have a hard time functioning normally and may lose touch with those closest to us.

Empowering Others

1. **Origin:** *"But each one must examine his own work, and then he will have reason for boasting in regard to himself alone, and not in regard to another. For each one will bear his own load. (Gal. 6:4-5 NASB)*
2. **Heartbeat:** We see from this Scripture that each person is ultimately responsible for his or her own life. We can't possibly help every person who is encumbered by life. With this in mind, we look to empower others to do what they never thought they could do on their own.
3. **Extreme—TAKING NO OWNERSHIP FOR OTHERS:** If we find ourselves never supporting those around us because we think they're "capable to do it on their own," we've strayed too far.

We've allowed our own perception to cut us off from actually loving our neighbor.

Balance: Love Abounding in Discernment

Philippians 1:9-10 (NASB) says, *"And this I pray, that your love may abound still more and more in real knowledge and all discernment, so that you may approve the things that are excellent, in order to be sincere and blameless until the day of Christ."* As stated above, we can't possibly take on everyone as our responsibility. We need to ask the Lord for who to help and when to help them. It takes discernment to know what's "not our deal" and what is. If we feel the Lord prompting us to help someone out, we should be obedient! On the other hand, if we genuinely feel Him saying, "Not this time," then we should let go of the situation and commit it to God in prayer. Our objective should always be to say and do what the Father is saying and doing. The more we lean on Him, the more clear this will become in our day to day walks.

Application: When it comes to helping people, there is no black and white rule book. Nevertheless, if you feel that you've been serving so many people that you yourself are exhausted and unable to truly live, then ask the Lord if there is someone you can empower to do more on their own. If you're on the other side of things and feel you aren't involved in very many people's lives, then get out there and find someone to help, love, and serve!

"The Holy Spirit will prompt us in the right direction as we learn to hear His voice and respond in obedience."
—*Crystal McDowell*

Day 52

God Is Holy vs. God Is Unconditional Love

God Is Holy

1. **Origin:** *"As obedient children, do not be conformed to the former lusts which were yours in your ignorance, but like the Holy One who called you, be holy yourselves also in all your behavior; because it is written, 'You shall be holy, for I am holy.'"* (1 Pet. 1:14-16. NASB)

2. **Heartbeat:** Throughout the Old and New Testament, we can see God establishing His holiness through His laws and structure. One of the great Biblical truths is that everything that is pure is in God and He is worthy of praise because of His purity and goodness.

3. **Extreme—LEGALISM:** We can take the realities of God's holiness to the extreme when we think we aren't able to present ourselves to Him when we make a mistake. We shouldn't view God as a taskmaster who demands holiness before we receive His enabling grace.

God Is Unconditional Love

1. **Origin:** *"The one who does not love does not know God, for God is love. By this the love of God was manifested in us, that God has sent His only begotten Son into the world so that we might live through Him."* (1 Jn. 4:8-9 NASB)

2. **Heartbeat:** Jesus is the purest example of love, shown when He paid the price so we could live in freedom from our sins. He loves the broken and lost and wants to meet us where we are.

He saw us in sin and still chose us while we were dead in it (See Ephesians 2:4-5).

3. **Extreme—GREASY GRACE:** We take advantage of God's unconditional love when we think that, because God loves us, it doesn't matter if we sin or have poor behavior. It is true that our conduct doesn't determine our salvation but, if we think it doesn't have any value, then we have missed the heart of God.

Balance: God Is All in All

God is holy and God is love. We can see God's value for sanctification and holiness in the Old Testament when He set up laws of purification before one could enter His presence. On the other hand, God loved us so much that He was willing to make the ultimate sacrifice of purification by sending His Son. This sacrifice enabled Him to go to the most broken people and places to restore them back to holiness. Holiness comes by grace through faith. This doesn't merely put righteousness in our account, it also enables us to live it out.

Application: Let God's love motivate you to be a living sacrifice, pleasing to Him. Christ has paid for your perfection and sees you as unblemished. Know that your salvation is never dependent on your ability to do something, it is dependent on Christ's ultimate sacrifice. Find time to take communion today. As you partake of the body and the blood, ask the Lord for a revelation of both His holiness *and* His lovingkindness.

"Holiness, as taught in the Scriptures, is not based upon knowledge on our part. Rather, it is based upon the resurrected Christ in-dwelling us and changing us into His likeness."
—A.W. Tozer

Day 53

Lifestyle of Encouragement vs. Lifestyle of Confrontation

Lifestyle of Encouragement

1. **Origin:** *"Let no corrupt word proceed out of your mouth, but what is good for necessary edification, that it may impart grace to the hearers." (Eph. 4:29)*
2. **Heartbeat:** Seeing others built up and edified is crucial to the Body of Christ. We need to encourage people and spur them on in their identity so they can grow all the more into God's calling for their lives.
3. **Extreme—AVOIDING CORRECTION:** Encouragement is important but, if we believe it's the only form of edification, we are in the wrong. If we're so fixed on encouraging and blessing people that we overlook error in their lives and never call them to a higher standard, then we've entered into an extreme.

Lifestyle of Confrontation

1. **Origin:** *"Listen to counsel and accept discipline, that you may be wise the rest of your days." (Prov. 19:20 NASB)*
2. **Heartbeat:** If we desire to see people grow, confronting issues in their behavior or beliefs is necessary. We don't want to let people walk around with "something in their teeth." We desire to see them live clean and free.
3. **Extreme—AVOIDING ENCOURAGEMENT:** It is dangerous and potentially damaging to only confront and correct people. Love and encouragement are necessary ingredients. If we are always seeing people's faults and never the "gold" within their lives, we need to shift our mindset.

Balance: Speak the Truth in Love

"But speaking the truth in love, we are to grow up in all aspects into Him who is the head, even Christ" (Eph. 4:15 NASB). When we speak the truth in love, we will find ourselves both confronting issues and encouraging hearts. Truth can look like a bold statement that prunes a prideful attitude, and it can also look like a gentle word that exhorts a person into their potential in Christ. The key is to do it in love. We need to assess each situation and ask the Lord what truth needs to be heard. Whether it's a truth that comforts or hurts, it will cause growth!

Application: It's time to speak the truth in love to those around you. That may look like an encouraging word or it may look like a confrontational one. Whatever the case, ask the Lord to fill your heart with love. Pray this prayer: *"Lord, You've given me truth as a sword and I intend to use it. I want to sculpt people into Your image. Lead me into situations that allow me to speak the truth in love that I might see lives transformed and changed. Amen."*

"If you look for truth, you may find comfort in the end; if you look for comfort you will not get either comfort or truth only soft soap and wishful thinking to begin, and in the end, despair."
—*C.S. Lewis*

Day 54

Abundance vs. Simple Living

Abundance

1. **Origin:** *"For you know the grace of our Lord Jesus Christ, that though He was rich, yet for your sakes He became poor, that you through His poverty might become rich. (2 Cor. 8:9)*
2. **Heartbeat:** When we have a desire to become rich, it often begins with a heart to serve God with our wealth. We see prosperity as a true gift included in the victory of the Cross.
3. **Extreme—LOVE OF MONEY:** We know we've gone too far with our riches when money takes the "God spot" in our focus. Because of the lure of wealth, some fall into the extreme of pursuing riches instead of pursuing the One who provides the riches.

Simple Living

1. **Origin:** *"If you want to be perfect, go, sell what you have and give to the poor, and you will have treasure in heaven; and come, follow Me." (Matt. 19:16-22)*
2. **Heartbeat:** With love in our hearts, we may desire to embrace a lifestyle of minimalism in order to more effectively follow Jesus. We are driven to let go of worldly things and to embrace the heavenly.
3. **Extreme—POVERTY:** If we have a strong conviction to be detached from material things, we may take it to the extreme and live intentionally in lack. We could be led to denying blessings from above without even realizing it.

Balance: Content in Christ

"I know how to get along with humble means, and I also know how to live in prosperity; in any and every circumstance I have learned the secret of being filled and going hungry, both of having abundance and suffering need. I can do all things through Him who strengthens me" (Phil. 4:12-13 NASB). God does desire that we live in abundance, but He doesn't desire that we be consumed by worldly riches. Wealth in itself isn't evil, but it is the "love" of money that is the root of all evil (see 1 Tim. 6:10). After all, those with no material possessions can still struggle with a lust for it. It's all about the contentment of our hearts. It's about our inner man being free from greed and satisfied with Christ.

Application: Do you find yourself in either category? Do you tend to run after money, or do you avoid the topic altogether? Ask the Lord to bring you into a healthy balance today when it comes to your finances. Read Philippians 4:12-13, as written above, and make it your prayer to be content with Him and all *He* has in store for you.

"The very nature of joy makes nonsense of our common distinction between having and wanting."
—C.S. Lewis

Day 55

Urgent Evangelism vs. Relational Evangelism

Urgent Evangelism

1. **Origin:** *"For if I preach the gospel, I have nothing to boast of, for necessity is laid upon me; yes, woe is me if I do not preach the gospel!" (1 Cor. 9:16)*
2. **Heartbeat:** There is a lost and dying world that needs to hear the Gospel of Jesus Christ. We are God's ambassadors and we are called to preach His Word.
3. **Extreme—LACK OF DEPTH AND COMPASSION:** If we spend little time connecting with people and all of our time preaching to them, then we've swung to an extreme. If you can quote John 3:16 to a woman in the grocery story, but cannot quote her name back to her, then you've potentially been more focused on the goal of evangelism than the person in front of you.

Relational Evangelism

1. **Origin:** *"Then it happened that as Jesus was reclining at the table in the house, behold, many tax collectors and sinners came and were dining with Jesus and His disciples." (Matt. 9:10 NASB)*
2. **Heartbeat:** Jesus was known as the friend of sinners. In the same way, we should have a heart to befriend those the world rejects, those that are lost and helpless. Connection is a necessary ingredient in seeing people come to Jesus.
3. **Extreme—COMFORTABILITY AND STAGNANCY:** If our friendships with the lost and unbelieving are yielding little transformative fruit, then it may be time to speak up about the Good News of Jesus. We cannot merely hang out with sinners

and give them loving attention; we need to also lead them to the hope we carry.

Balance: Be the Light

"You are the light of the world. A city that is set on a hill cannot be hidden" (Matt. 5:14). If we let our light shine before all men, we will live in balance. We will have opportunities to both connect with people and preach the Good News of Jesus! If we simply abide in God's light and walk in His love, people will want what we have. We won't always have to step in and ask if we can share a word with them; they will see the hope within us and ask us what's so different about us. The world is drawn to light; the more you shine, the more relationships you will build. Certainly, there are many good times to boldly preach the Word, but don't let your urgency cause you to overlook how you're coming across.

Application: Take a look at your relationships. Have you been wearing some of your friends out with your zealous heart to share Jesus with them? Or are you on the other side; have they never heard you mention His name? Whatever the case may be, it's time to step into balance and watch God do something miraculous. If you've felt overly urgent, take up some small talk with your friends and/or family and have fun. If you've never shared Jesus with them, take a step and expect something big!

"Any method of evangelism will work if God is in it."
—Leonard Ravenhill

CONCLUSION

We pray that this book has been helpful in pointing you to Christ and that it has empowered you to live a balanced life. We encourage you to re-read pages that you feel you still need clarity on. If you ever feel like you keep veering into an extreme, take a risk and do something out of your norm, even if it's uncomfortable! Take hold of the truth and let it transform you from the inside out. The more you allow His Word to come into your heart and your mind, the more you will embody its reality. Keep going to the Lord in prayer and allow His Word to center you in His perfect will. Pursue Truth Himself and He will guide you into all truth. Bless you in the abundance of God's grace!

"Now may the God of hope fill you with all joy and peace in
believing, that you may abound in hope by
the power of the Holy Spirit."
—Romans 15:13